嘻哈口语
大话校园

Everyday Dialogues on Campus

[英] Nick Stirk 著

张满胜 译

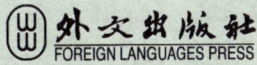
FOREIGN LANGUAGES PRESS

Introduction

These dialogues will make you laugh, make you cry, make you think but most of all they will make your English better. Each chapter has four topics that are connected to its main theme. Each of the topics contains three dialogues. There is brief background information on each topic which is relevant to students lives here in China. They are special in three ways.

First, they have been written by a native speaker who has had several years experience in China teaching at top universities. They are full of upto-date natural expressions used by native speakers, which means that you will be using the same language that they speak.

Second, there is an emphasis on collocations, phrases and expressions. This is because two, three, four and even five-word collocations, phrases and expressions make up a huge percentage of all naturally-occurring text, spoken or written. We are more likely to memorise and use phrases rather than single words. So get rid of word lists and replace them with lists of phrases.

Third, and most important of all, these dialogues are close to students' lives and represent common experiences that they would encounter daily.

I wish to acknowledge the encouragement and assistance provided by my publisher Cai Qing. I would like to thank my English majors (classes 06701, 06702, 06703) at Beijing University of Posts and Telecom-munications for their help in road-testing these dialogues and for making many valuable suggestions. I would specially like to thank Li Yang for her suggestions on various dialogues. I am truly grateful for her insight and knowledge of campus life.

本书中的对话会让你哭，让你笑，让你思考，最主要的是会让你的英语有所长进。每章内容都包含四个话题，与本章主旨密切相关。每个话题含有三个对话。每章前都有背景信息的介绍。

特别之处有三：

其一，本书的作者来自英国，并且拥有多年在中国一流大学的教学经验。对话中充满了最时尚的表达方式，也就是说，你将会学到现在英国最流行的口语。

其二，对话中突出强调了词组、短语和表达法。因为在任何课文中，无论是口语还是书面语，由二、三、四、甚至是五个单词所组成的词组、短语和表达法都占据了主要部分。所以，在学习英语时，不要只记单个单词，而应该记忆词组和短语。

第三，也是最重要的，这些对话紧密贴近学生生活，取材来自生活，原汁原味，是日常英语会话中所必须。

非常感谢我的出版人蔡菁小姐给予我的鼓励与帮助。感谢北京邮电大学英语系的同学（他们是06701、06702和06703班）为本书中的对话进行了实际演练，并提出了很多宝贵的意见。我要特别感谢李杨为对话提出了许多中肯的建议，以及她对校园生活的丰富见解。

How to Get the Most out of These Dialogues 使用指南

Role play dialogues are excellent opportunities for learners of English to practice English because they give students the chance to assume a role that is not their own. They can be anyone they want. It does not matter if you make a mistake because it is not you who makes it. It is your character who does! You can totally assume the character and personality of your part and play it to the hilt and beyond! Your voice and actions can be completely over the top and yet it does not matter because it is only acting. Role playing is a safe and enjoyable way to learn English. It is a good idea to find a partner to practice the following dialogues with.

Tips on role plays

1. Don't be afraid to act the part
2. Try to get into the character
3. Explore different voices
4. Use appropriate movements and gestures
5. Change parts so that you can play a different character
6. Don't be afraid to play a character of the opposite sex

Studying spoken English really can be easy, even in a fast-paced and demanding world. Take this book with you on the go. As each dialogue is independent of the others, you can study them piece by piece. Take the 15 minutes you're stuck in traffic to read a topic. Carry it with you on the subway. Squeeze in a few minutes here and there. If you practice one dialogue a day then at the end of 50 days you'll be amazed at how your English has grown. Your confidence in speaking will be sky high and when a foreigner appears you will have plenty to talk about!

对于英语学习者来说，在英语会话中进行角色扮演是锻炼英语水平的一个绝好的机会，这让学生们有机会去担任一个完全不同于自己本人的任何角色。即使犯了错误也无所谓，因为并不是你犯的，是你扮演的角色犯下的！你完全可以设想自己所扮演角色的性格特征并将其发挥到极至。你的声音、动作都可以很夸张，这并没有什么，不过是在演戏罢了。角色扮演是一个安全并且令人愉快的英语学习方式。找个搭档与你一起练习书中的对话，是个不错的主意。

角色扮演小贴士

1. 表演时不必有任何顾虑
2. 努力融入角色
3. 语言表达要抑扬顿挫
4. 使用恰当的肢体动作和手势
5. 进行角色互换，以便尝试不同角色
6. 不要羞于扮演异性角色

学习口语其实很简单，即使在这个快节奏、竞争激烈的社会里。随身带着这本书，书中每段对话都是相互独立的，你可以逐一学习。路上堵车15分钟，你不妨就来读一个话题。坐地铁时也带着它，四处挤点时间就够了。要是你每天练习一篇对话，50天后你就会惊讶于自己英语的进步。你在讲英语时会非常有信心，再遇到老外的时候，你就不会无话可说了。

Contents 目录

Chapter 1 Love 爱情
1. Looking for Love 寻找爱情 / 1
2. Courtship 恋爱阶段 / 8
3. Pure Love 纯真的爱情 / 14
4. Breaking up 恋人分手 / 21

Chapter 2 Leisure 休闲时光
5. Night Life 夜生活 / 28
6. Student Activities on Campus 校园里的学生活动 / 34
7. Music and Movies 音乐与电影 / 41
8. Keeping Fit 保持健康 / 48

Chapter 3 Shopping 购物
9. Clothes 服装 / 54
10. Malls and Supermarkets 购物广场与超市 / 60
11. Street Markets 街边市场 / 66
12. Online Shopping 网上购物 / 73

Chapter 4 Campus 大学校园
13. Dorm Life 宿舍生活 / 80
14. Classes 课程 / 86
15. Campus 校园 / 92
16. Health 健康 / 97

Chapter 5 Family and Friends 家庭和朋友
17. One-child Family 独生子女家庭 / 104
18. Parents and Children 父母和孩子 / 110
19. Extended Family 大家庭 / 117
20. Friends 朋友 / 124

Chapter 6　Travel 旅游
21. Public Transport　公共交通 / 131
22. Mainland China　中国大陆 / 138
23. Hong Kong, Macao and Taiwan　香港、澳门和台湾 / 145
24. Abroad　出国 / 152

Chapter 7　Student Activities 学生活动
25. Student Union　学生会 / 159
26. Sports　运动 / 166
27. Lost and Found　丢东西 / 173
28. Beijing 2008 Olympics　北京2008奥运会 / 180

Chapter 8　Learning English 英语学习
29. Speaking　口语 / 187
30. Writing　写作 / 194
31. Reading　阅读 / 202
32. Listening　听力 / 208

Chapter 9　Finance 金融财务
33. Managing on a Budget　预算管理 / 215
34. Banks and Credit Cards　银行和信用卡 / 222
35. Scholarships　奖学金 / 229
36. The Stock Market　股票市场 / 236

Chapter 10　Career 事业
37. Internships　实习 / 242
38. Part-time Jobs　兼职工作 / 249
39. Running a Part-time Business　边上学边做生意 / 255
40. Finding a Job　找工作 / 262

Chapter 1　Love 爱情

1　寻找爱情
Looking for Love

Background Information

A survey by the Guangdong Youth Development Report in early January 2007 found that loneliness is the most important motivator for falling in love on campus. A survey by Shanghai iResearch Co. found that
- 80% accept finding partners online
- 70% think the Internet provides more opportunities to make friends
- 50% think their social activities are too few to find a partner
- 60% are doubtful about matchmaking websites

2007年1月，广东青年发展报告的调查显示，孤独感是导致校园恋爱的最主要诱因。上海iResearch公司的一项调查发现：
- 80%的受访者能够接受网上寻友。
- 70%的受访者认为互联网为结交朋友提供了更多的机会。
- 50%的受访者认为他们的社交活动太少了，以至于不能够找到恋爱对象。
- 60%的受访者对婚介网站持怀疑态度。

背景信息

Dialogue 1

Julia: Betty, I really need your help. I've met this boy on the Internet who I really like.

Betty: How did you get to know him?

J: Through QQ. We just started chatting and soon found out that we had a lot in common.

B: So tell me more about him.

J: Well he's 20 and works for a company in Shenzhen. He also phones me and I like the sound of his voice.

B: That's a good start but don't forget you're in Wuhan and you've never met him.

J: I know but I think of him every day and I get really depressed when he doesn't call. I've really developed a big **crush**① on him.

B: But that may be all it is. Just a crush. You can't fall in love with someone you've never met!

J: But every day is so special because of him. I just **can't get him off my mind**② and my studies are suffering.

B: I think you really need to **get a grip**③. If you are going to fall in love with someone then you need to stop living in a dream world and find a real person. You should socialize more and then the right person will come along.

J: What if I invited him to come here to Wuhan?

B: That's a good idea. Then you could find out, **once and for all**④, whether you like each other or not.

J: I'll send him a message tonight!

习惯用语 1

① crush: 对某人一时的迷恋（该词后边通常接介词 on）
② can't get sb. off one's mind: 无法忘记某人，总是想着某人
③ get a grip: 恢复理智
④ once and for all: 坚决地，断然地（做出决定）

J: Betty,我需要你的帮助。我在网上遇到个男孩,我真的很喜欢他!
B: 你是怎么认识他的?
J: 通过 QQ。刚开始,我们就是毫无目的的闲聊,但很快我们发现彼此有很多共同的地方。
B: 那给我讲讲他的情况。
J: 他 20 岁,在深圳的一家公司工作。他还常给我打电话,我很喜欢他的声音。
B: 开端不错,但是别忘了你在武汉,而且你从没有见过他。
J: 这我知道,可我每天都在想他,而且他不给我打电话的时候,我就会很沮丧。我已经彻底迷上他了。
B: 这也许不过是一时冲动罢了,你又没见过他,你怎么可能爱上他呢?
J: 可是由于他的存在,每天都变得很特别。我满脑子想着的都是他,总也挥之不去,这都影响我的学习了。
B: 我认为你真的需要恢复理智。如果你打算恋爱,那就得活的现实点儿,不要整天做白日梦,找一个现实中的人来爱。要多交际,这样到时你的如意郎君自然就会出现了。
J: 我邀请他来武汉,怎么样?
B: 这主意不错,那样你就可以彻彻底底搞清楚是否真的彼此喜欢对方了。
J: 我今晚就给他发信息!

Questions 1

1. Have you ever chatted to someone on the Internet who you've developed a romantic interest in?
2. Do you think the Internet is a good way of finding a partner?

Dialogue 2

Hilary: Hi Catherine. How's life?
Catherine: Everything's great! How are you and Kevin?
H: We're fine too. You should find a boyfriend and then we all could go out on dates together.

C: Not for me! I think campus love is a waste of time. I'd rather be studying.

H: But studying all the time is so boring! You need to enjoy life while you're here. I know I do.

C: You know my parents have sacrificed a lot for me to come here. They want me to do well. How will they feel if they hear that I'm spending most of my time with my boyfriend instead of my textbooks!

H: Hey come on! It's not like that! Kevin and I often study together. There's more to life here than dorm, classroom, library, canteen and dorm again!

C: No pains, no gains! It will be worth it all in the end.

H: You ought to seriously consider that never again in your life will you be surrounded by so many **eligible bachelors**①. It's a once in a lifetime opportunity!

C: Love can wait. I'm too young to have my heart broken. When I've taken the first few steps on my **career ladder**② then I'll start looking for a soul mate.

H: You old **dinosaur**③ you! By then all the best guys will have been taken. You'll end up an **old maid**④!

C: Don't care! Not worried! After all tomorrow is another day!

H: Yes and you'll end up with no happy memories of your time here!

C: Do you want to go to the library?

H: Only if Kevin can come!

习惯用语 2

① eligible bachelors: 会成为好丈夫的单身男士
② career ladder: 在公司或职业发展方面的晋升
③ dinosaur: 跟不上潮流的人（这不同于我们汉语里用"恐龙"表示相貌丑陋的人）
④ old maid: 老处女

H: 你好 Catherine。最近怎么样？

C: 很不错！你和 Kevin 怎么样？

H: 我们也很好。你应该找个男朋友，到时候我们就可以一起出去玩儿了。

C: 我才不呢！我觉得上学期间谈恋爱完全是浪费时间。我宁可用那时间去学习。

H: 但总是学习也太无聊了！你得学会享受校园里的生活，就像我一样。

C: 你知道吗，为了能让我来这里学习，我的父母付出了很多。他们希望我能够有所作为。要是他们知道我把大量的时间都花在男友身上而不是用来学习，那会是什么心情？

H: 得了吧，没有那么夸张！Kevin 和我经常在一起学习。生活不仅仅是宿舍、教室、图书馆、食堂、再回到宿舍，这样周而复始。

C: 没有付出就没有收获。我这样努力学习最终会有回报的，是值得的。

H: 你得好好考虑一下了，在你的一生中，再也不会像现在这样，身边有这么多的单身好男人了。这是一生才有一次的机会啊！

C: 谈恋爱还可以再等等。我还太小，难以承受心灵的创伤。当我的事业已经开始稳步发展的时候，我就会开始找寻我的另一半。

H: 你简直就是个老古董！到那时候所有的男孩都"名草有主"了，你就只有当老处女的份儿了！

C: 那有什么？甭着急。明天又是崭新的一天，机会有的是！

H: 是，你到时也不会有大学校园里的美好回忆！

C: 你现在想去图书馆吗？

H: Kevin 去我就去。

Questions 2

1. Do you think campus love is a good thing? Why? Why not?
2. Have your studies been affected by having a boyfriend/girlfriend?

Dialogue 3

Mandy: What do you think I should look for in a boyfriend?

Cherry: Depends on whether you take the traditional view or the modern view.

M: OK. Tell me what the traditional view is first.

C: Well, he should be older than you, taller than you, better educated than you and richer than you!

M: That sounds OK but what if I don't love him?

C: Then we move on to the modern view. You fall in love with someone and it doesn't matter whether he's younger than you, smaller than you, less educated than you or poorer than you!

M: But I want to have a comfortable life so he has to be richer than me! After all, **no money; no honey**[①]!

C: Do you mind if he's smaller than you?

M: Of course I mind. I don't want to marry a **midget**[②]! I want to look up to him, not look down on him!

C: What if he's less educated than you?

M: We'd have nothing to talk about!

C: What if he's younger than you?

M: Too immature. He'd only be interested in sport and computer games!

C: Well, now at least you know what to look for in a boyfriend!

习惯用语 3

① no money; no honey: 没有钱就不会找到爱人
② midget: 侏儒

M: 你觉得我应该找个什么样的男朋友?
C: 那得看你的个人恋爱观了，是传统的还是现代的。
M: 嗯，你先说说传统恋爱观指的都是什么。

C：传统观念就是，他应该年龄比你大，个头比你高，受教育程度比你好，也比你有钱。
M：听起来不错，可我要是不喜欢他怎么办？
C：那我们就来看看现代恋爱观了。你爱上了一个人，即使他年龄比你小，个头比你矮，受教育程度比你低，比你贫穷，也无所谓。
M：可我不想过苦日子，所以他应该比我富有。毕竟，"贫贱夫妻百事哀"嘛！
C：那你介意他个头比你矮吗？
M：当然介意了！我可不想跟侏儒结婚！我想仰望他，而不是俯视他。
C：要是他的受教育程度比你低呢？
M：那我们就不会有共同语言了！
C：要是他年龄比你小呢？
M：那他就不成熟，只会对运动和电脑游戏感兴趣。
C：你看，至少现在你知道该找一个什么样的男朋友了吧。

Questions 3

1. What do you look for in a boyfriend?
2. Would you take the traditional view or the modern view? Why?

Chapter 1　Love 爱情

2　恋爱阶段
Courtship

Background Information

Courtship is the process of attracting another for an intimate relationship leading to marriage. It may take days, weeks, months and even years.

In the West there are several steps involved in courtship. First, the man would woo the girl, that is, seek to win her affections. Then would come a period of going out together. Finally, the man would propose to her. Traditionally, the man would go on bended knee, say, "I love you. Will you marry me?" And give her a diamond ring. They would then be engaged to marry.

两人恋爱拍拖可能会花费几天、几周、几个月、甚至是好几年的时间，这是异性之间彼此吸引、卿卿我我、亲密无间的一段美好时期，是为将来准备结婚的。

在西方，恋爱会分为几个阶段。首先，男士要追求女士，就是要赢得她的芳心。然后就进入了约会期。最后，男士会向女士求婚。通常男士会单膝跪地，对女方说："我爱你，愿意嫁给我吗？"然后献上一枚钻戒。之后两人就订婚并准备结婚。

背景信息

Dialogue 1

Tony: William, can I ask your advice?

William: Sure, go ahead.

T: There's a girl in our class that I really like but I always feel shy in her presence. My face turns red, my heart beats faster and I get **tongue-tied**①.

W: I know what you mean! Do you want to **ask her out**②?

T: Of course I do! But how?

W: Do you think she likes you? That's the first thing you need to find out.

T: Yeah, but how? I can't go up to her and ask her that!

W: Does she notice you when you're in the same room? Is there a lot of eye contact? Does she smile at you? Does she talk to you?

T: I don't think she even knows that I'm alive!

W: You've got a tough job ahead of you, then! You need to get her to notice you.

T: Easier said than done!

W: Start by being friendly with her. Chat with her. **Pay her compliments**③. Try to **act natural**④.

T: I'll try.

W: Let me know what happens, OK?

T: OK.

习惯用语 1

① tongue-tied：（由于胆怯、难堪等）说不出话的
② ask sb. out：男女约会
③ pay sb. compliments：赞美或恭维某人
④ act natural：表现自然

T: William，给我些建议好吗？
W: 当然可以，说吧。
T: 我们班里有个女孩，我真的很喜欢她，可是在她面前，我总是很

害羞，脸会变红，心跳加速，然后就变得口齿不伶，说不出话来。
W: 我明白你的意思了。你想和她约会吧？
T: 当然想了！可是该怎么做呢？
W: 你觉得她喜欢你吗？这是你首先需要搞清楚的事情。
T: 可是我该怎么做？我总不能走到她面前直接去问吧！
W: 你们俩同处一室的时候，她会注意到你吗？是否有目光交流呢？她对你微笑吗？她跟你说话吗？
T: 我觉得她根本就不知道这个世界上有我的存在。
W: 那你需要面对的一个艰巨任务就是要引起她的注意。
T: 说得容易！
W: 跟她从普通朋友开始做起，与她聊天，适当地赞美她，一切都要显得很自然。
T: 好吧，我试试。
W: 到时告诉我进展情况，好吗？
T: 好的。

Questions 1

1. Are you shy with the opposite sex?
2. How do you get girls to notice you?
3. Do you ever ask someone's advice about romance?

Dialogue 2

Anna: Kathy, what would you do if there was a boy you liked?
Kathy: You mean, if I wanted to be his girlfriend?
A: Yeah, would you wait for him to ask you out or would you **make the first move**[①]?
K: I would definitely wait for him to ask me first!
A: Why? What difference does it make? We're equal now you know.
K: Not in this, we're not! Men are like hunters. They like to chase girls.
A: But that's the problem! He's not chasing me!

K: Well, you can't chase him! Men don't like that.
A: Why not?
K: Because even if you get together he won't respect you. He'll think you're **easy**②.
A: But I'm not.
K: Makes no difference. As soon as he **gets what he wants**③ he'll **dump you**④.
A: I see. So I have to wait for him to make the first move even if it takes him a million years!
K: **'Fraid**⑤ so. But you could act friendly towards him and he may **get the message**⑥.
A: OK, I'll try that and see what happens!

习惯用语2

① make the first move: 主动约某人，主动出击
② easy: 这里指一个轻易就跟别人上床的女孩
③ gets what he wants: 发生性关系
④ dump you: 结束恋情，甩掉对方，抛弃对方
⑤ 'Fraid: afraid 的缩写形式
⑥ get the message: 了解对方的意图，暗示

A: Kathy，要是有个你喜欢的男孩，你会怎么做？
K: 你是说，如果我想成为他的女朋友？
A: 是的，你会等他来约你，还是主动出击，去约他？
K: 我当然会等他先来约我了！
A: 为什么？这有什么区别吗？现在男女都平等了。
K: 在这方面可不是。男人就像猎手，他们喜欢追求女孩。
A: 可问题是，他没有追求我！
K: 那你也不能去追他！男人不喜欢那样。
A: 为什么不能？
K: 因为即使你们在一起了，他也不会尊重你。他会觉得你是个轻易就到手的女孩。
A: 可我不是啊。

K: 这毫无关系。一旦得到了他想要的，他就会抛弃你。
A: 噢，就是说，我要一直等到他主动开口，即使是一百万年也要等。
K: 恐怕是。但你可以友好地接近他，那样他也许会得到一些暗示。
A: 好吧，我试试，看效果究竟如何。

Questions 2

1. Would you ever ask a boy out? Why? Why not?
2. Do you prefer to chase girls?
3. What would you do if a girl asked you out?

Dialogue 3

William: Well, any news?
Tony: Yeah, I finally asked Anna out!
W: Great! She said yes I hope?
T: Of course! How could she **resist my manly charms**①!
W: How did you do it? What did you say?
T: Well, I did everything you suggested like being friendly to her and talking with her and....
W: Come on! **Cut to the chase**②!
T: OK! OK! I was going to class when I saw her on her own so I went up to her and asked if she wanted to go with me to the cinema sometime. And she said yes!
W: Congratulations!
T: Thanks, but we're not officially boyfriend and girlfriend yet. We're going tomorrow night.
W: What kind of film are you going to see?
T: A horror film.
W: Why on earth go to see a horror film?
T: Someone once told me that girls get really scared and don't mind if you put your arms around them.
W: You **Casanova**③ you!

习惯用语 3

① resist sb.'s manly charms: 抵挡某人的男性魅力
② cut to the chase: 切重要点
③ Casanova: 卡萨诺瓦（1725－1798，意大利冒险家，以所写的包括他的许多风流韵事的《自传》而著称）。风流浪子，好色之徒。

W: 最近有什么新进展吗？
T: 是的，我终于约了 Anna！
W: 太棒了！她同意了，对吧？
T: 当然了！凭我的男子魅力，她怎么能拒绝呢！
W: 你是怎么做到的？都说了些什么？
T: 就是按照你的建议做的，比如与她友好地接触，主动跟她聊天什么的。
W: 行了，赶紧说重点吧！
T: 好的，好的！就是有一天我去教室上课，在路上正好看到她是一个人，我就走过去问她要是有时间的话，是否愿意与我一起看电影。然后她就同意了！
W: 太好了！祝贺啊！
T: 谢啦！但我们还不是真正的男女朋友关系。我们约着明晚一起去看电影。
W: 那你打算带她去看什么类型的电影？
T: 当然是恐怖片啦。
W: 干嘛非要去看恐怖片啊？
T: 我记得有人跟我说过，当女孩害怕的时候，你趁机伸手去搂着她，她是不会介意的。
W: 你个大色狼！

Questions 3

1. How would you ask a girl out?
2. What would you do if she said no?
3. Where would you take her for your first date?

Chapter 1　Love 爱情

3　纯真的爱情
Pure Love

Background Information

Many students say that their time at university is when they can experience pure love. This is a time when love is innocent when two people come together for love, rather than a house, car or a good job. There are no pressures from parents to get married as they are still young. It is a time when they can choose who they love and how they love away from outside pressure. Even though the relationship may break up it will bring sweet memories in later years.

很多学生都说，只有在大学期间才能经历真正纯真的爱情，因为在此期间，爱是非常纯粹的，两人走到一起完全是因为爱，而不是因为别的原因比如房子、车子，或是好的工作等等。由于还年轻，他们也不会受到来自父母的要求结婚的压力。他们可以不受外界的压力去选择自己爱的对象和爱的方式。即使最终两人分手了，这期间的爱情也会给以后带来甜蜜的回忆。

背景信息

Dialogue 1

Wayne: You'll never guess what my girlfriend gave me on Valentine's Day!

Paul: Flowers, chocolates, DVD, a scarf?

W: No, **nothing so mundane**①! It was a **memorable token**② of her love.

P: Can I see it, then?

W: No, but I can tell you about it. We were walking along Wangfujing when she suddenly said, "Let's play a game. See who can reach the end of the street first."

P: What a stupid idea for a game! It's obvious that you'd win.

W: Of course I was the hare to her tortoise! When I looked back she was far behind. But then she started screaming.

P: Screaming! What had happened?

W: She was shouting, "Stop thief! Catch him!"

P: Oh no! What happened next?

W: Two guys suddenly seized me and shouted, "Give it back to her!" I was so scared I could only say, "I'm not a thief."

P: You poor guy! What a terrible thing to happen!

W: When my girlfriend came up to me the two guys asked her, "What did he steal from you?" And you know what she said?

P: No, come on tell me!

W: My heart. He's stolen my heart.

P: She must love you very much.

W: Yeah, I'm very lucky to have a girlfriend like her.

习惯用语 1

① nothing so mundane: 不寻常的东西
② memorable token: 难忘的纪念品

W: 你绝对猜不到我女朋友送给我的情人节礼物是什么!
P: 花、巧克力、DVD,还是围巾?
W: 别这么庸俗!是一个代表她爱情的,很有意义的纪念品。
P: 我能看看吗?
W: 不能,不过我可以给你描述一下。当时我们正在王府井逛街,她突然说:"咱们来做个游戏吧,看看谁能先到街的那一头。"
P: 也太傻了吧?显然是你赢啊!
W: 那当然了,跟她这个小乌龟比起来,我就是一只兔子。我回头看的时候,发现她被远远的甩在了后面。然后,她就开始大声尖叫。
P: 尖叫?怎么回事儿?
W: 她喊到:"抓小偷!抓住他!"
P: 天哪!不是吧?那然后呢?
W: 两个男的突然抓住了我,还冲我吼到:"把东西还给她!"我当时吓坏了,只能说:"我不是小偷。"
P: 可怜的家伙!这叫什么事儿啊!
W: 我女朋友追上来以后,那两个家伙问她:"他偷你什么了?"你猜她说什么?
P: 不知道,赶紧说吧!别卖关子了!
W: 我的心。她说我偷了她的心!
P: 看来她一定是非常爱你!
W: 是啊,能有这样一个女孩做女朋友,我真的太幸运了!

Questions 1

1. What's the most memorable Valentine's Day gift you've ever received or given?
2. How will you spend Valentine's Day?

Dialogue 2

Sunny: How long have Ben and you been **going out**[①] now?
Ann: Over a year now. He really makes me happy.
S: I've noticed that but tell me more! How?
A: He likes to go shopping with me even though he hates it.
S: He must love you then!
A: Yeah and I like the way he cares for me. The little things he does for me. He always opens the door for me. He buys me flowers every week. He calls me every night to make certain I get enough sleep.
S: You certainly make a handsome couple! Aren't you afraid he'll fall in love with someone else?
A: No! He once told me that everyone should choose their love and love their choice. And that he had chosen me and would love me for ever.
S: What was the most romantic thing he has ever done?
A: It was on Valentine's Day. He sent me a message saying to meet me at the lake. When I got there I was surprised to see hundreds of red ribbons tied to the trees and bushes. I went up to one and looked at it closely. There was writing on it.
S: What did it say?
A: Ann I love you!
S: What did you do then?
A: I looked at some of the others. They all said the same thing. I just had to sit down and cry. I was so happy!
S: It must have taken him hours to do that. You are very lucky!

习惯用语 2

① go out: 谈恋爱，男女交往

S: 你和 Ben 交往多久了?
A: 到现在有一年多了。跟他在一起我很快乐。
S: 我注意到了。可他是怎么做的? 跟我说说。
A: 尽管他不喜欢逛商场,但他却愿意跟我一起逛。
S: 这说明他很爱你!
A: 是的,我很喜欢他体贴我的方式。有很多细节,比如他为我开门,每周都给我买花,他每天晚上都给我打电话,嘱咐我早点睡觉。
S: 你们简直太恩爱了! 你不怕他移情别恋吗?
A: 不怕。他跟我说过,每个人都有选择爱的权力,爱我所爱,无怨无悔。他说他既然选择了我,就会永远爱我。
S: 他所做过的最浪漫的事情是什么?
A: 那是一次情人节,他发来短信说要在湖边见面,当我到那里的时候,我惊奇地看到上百条红丝带系满了树梢。我走上前去,仔细看,上面还写着东西。
S: 写着什么?
A: Ann,我爱你!
S: 你当时是什么反应?
A: 我又看了看其他的丝带,都写着这句话。我都不知道如何是好了,就坐在地上哭了起来,我简直太高兴了!
S: 他肯定花了很多时间来办这件事,你太有福气了!

Questions 2

1. How does your bf show his love for you?
2. What's the most romantic thing he's done for you?

Dialogue 3

Denny: How's it going with Lena?

Robbie: Can't complain. She really cares about me.

D: You're always together. If I see one of you I'm bound to see the other! It's as if you are **joined at the hip**[①]!

R: We try to see each other as much as possible but it's not all whispering sweet nothings[2] in each other's ears you know!

D: **Pull the other one. It's got bells on!**[3]

R: It's true! Lena is really sensible. She insists on us studying together and always makes sure that I revise and do my homework.

D: Sounds like she's got you **under her thumb**[4]!

R: Not at all! It's just that she wants me to do well. She's thinking of the future.

D: Do I hear wedding bells?

R: Not yet! We're too young to get married.

D: But if you were old enough, would you?

R: Yes, **like a shot**[5]!

D: And would she?

R: Yes.

D: Don't forget to invite me to the wedding!

R: Don't worry, I won't!

习惯用语 3

① join at the hip: 一对形影不离的恋人
② whispering sweet nothings: 恋人间喃喃而语，卿卿我我
③ Pull the other one. It's got bells on! 开玩笑!
④ under sb.'s thumb: 在某人的支配下
⑤ like a shot: 立刻，马上

D: 你跟 Lena 怎么样了？
R: 非常好。她特别关心我。
D: 你们俩总是粘在一起。只要我看见你们中一个就肯定会看见另一个。真是形影不离啊！
R: 我们只是尽可能多与对方在一起，但并不总是卿卿我我的，这你是知道的。
D: 你别逗了！
R: 真的！Lena 特别明智。她总是强调我们要在一起学习，还总是关

心我是否在复习和做功课。
D: 怎么听起来你像是在被她管治着呀!
R: 才不是呢! 她只是希望我能很出色,她这是在为我们的未来考虑啊。
D: 这么说你们打算结婚了?
R: 没有! 我们还太年轻。
D: 但如果你们到了适婚年龄,你会娶她吗?
R: 当然了,马上就娶!
D: 那她会嫁给你吗?
R: 会的。
D: 结婚可不要忘了请我喝喜酒啊!
R: 放心,我一定邀请你!

Questions 3

1. Do you have a sensible girlfriend who can manage studies and romance?
2. Do you think that your romance will end in marriage? Why? Why not?

Chapter **1**   Love 爱 情

4 恋人分手
Breaking up

Background Information

There comes a time in most couples' lives when a break-up seems inevitable. What causes it and how to handle it puts a lot of stress and strain on a young person's shoulders. A survey by Sina.com found that 46% of students in relationships ended them upon graduation. In other words, nearly half of those who found pure love didn't want it to continue after university. Whatever the reasons for breaking up students with broken hearts have to learn to pick up the pieces, put them back together and proceed with their lives.

对大多数大学生恋人来说，分手似乎是一个难免的结局。是什么原因导致分手以及如何面对分手，这都给年轻人带来压力，造成痛苦，这可谓是压在年轻人肩上的重担。新浪网的一份调查显示，46%的学生恋人在毕业时就会分手。换句话说，将近一半的人在大学里找到了真爱，却并不想在毕业后延续这份爱。不论导致他们分手的原因是什么，遭受失恋痛苦的年轻学子们，都得学会捡拾起破碎的心，重新拼装起来，并继续前行，因为生活仍然在继续。

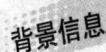
背景信息

Dialogue 1

Ella: Michelle, why are you crying?

Michelle: It's Andy. We've broken up.

E: Not again! How many times is that now?

M: I've lost count! Why is he so possessive and jealous?

E: There's nothing worse than a guy suffering from the **green-eyed monster**[①]! I know that in one way it shows he cares about you but he's acting like a prison warder and you're his prisoner!

M: I know but I always end up going back to him after a few days after he calls and apologises and sends me flowers. But I really can't keep on like this!

E: What was it about this time?

M: We were in the canteen having dinner and I saw a classmate and went over to talk to him for a few minutes about some student union activities we were both involved in. When I went back to Andy he was really upset, stormed out of the canteen and later called me to say we were finished.

E: Well as long as you keep going back to him he'll carry on behaving like this.

M: But you know I'm really fond of him although I don't like this kind of behaviour.

E: What you should do is **call his bluff**[②]. Tell him that he has to change his behaviour or you will walk out of his life for good. Give him a month during which you won't see him or contact him.

M: Drastic measures for a drastic situation, right?

E: Yeah, and who knows, after a month you might not miss him at all!

习惯用语 1

① green-eyed monster: 嫉妒
② call sb.'s bluff: 接受挑战，迫使某人兑现他恫吓人的假话

E: Michelle，你怎么哭了？

M: 我和 Andy 分手了。

E: 又分了？你们都分了多少回了？

M: 我也记不清了！他怎么占有欲那么强，那么爱嫉妒啊？

E: 是啊，没有什么比一个爱吃醋的男人更可怕了！我知道，一方面这说明他关心你，但另一方面也说明他想要牢牢地看住你，就像狱警看着犯人那样。

M: 我知道，可是每次他给我打电话、道歉、送花之后，没几天，我就又回到他身边了。但我真的无法再这样下去了！

E: 你们这回是因为什么？

M: 我们当时正在食堂吃饭，我看见一个同学，就过去跟他聊了聊我们共同参与的一些学生会的活动。我回来后，发现 Andy 特别生气，随后他气冲冲地走了，之后就给我打电话说我们完了。

E: 你要知道啊，要是你这次再回到他身边，他下次还会这样妒忌的。

M: 可我真的很喜欢他，尽管我不太喜欢他的这种做法。

E: 你这次就应该跟他来真的了，他不是说分手嘛，就跟他分好了。你就跟他说，他必须改改自己的这些毛病，否则你就会永远离开他，再也不回头了。给他一个月的时间，在这期间，你不要见他，也不要与他联系。

M: 非常情况，非常处理，对吗？

E: 对，说不定，一个月之后你根本就把他忘了呢！

Questions 1

1. Do you have a possessive boyfriend or girlfriend?
2. How do you react to that kind of behaviour?

Dialogue 2

Vivian: Oh, Carol I've just found out that Michael has been cheating on me!

Carol: The **love rat**①! What are you going to do?

V: Obviously I'm going to dump him. What else can I do!

C: Yeah, once a cheat, always a cheat is what I say!

V: But I still have feelings for him.

C: You are bound to have after being with him for a long time but those feelings will fade in time.

V: I hope so. But I still miss him. What should I do?

C: I know! Let's **pay him back**②!

V: You mean revenge? How?

C: Yeah. By getting you fixed up with someone else!

V: But who?

C: I have a friend at another university. He's **drop-dead gorgeous**③! I'll call him and see if I can arrange a date for Friday.

V: Friday? But our class party is that night!

C: Yeah and Michael will be there!

V: So while Michael's expecting me to be crying my eyes out in the dorm I'll turn up with this **dishy guy**④ and he'll be the one crying his eyes out!

C: That's **girl power**⑤ babe!

习惯用语 2

① love rat: 欺骗女生感情的人
② pay sb. back: 得到报应
③ drop-dead gorgeous: 非常帅气（非常漂亮）
④ dishy guy: 很有魅力的男人
⑤ girl power: 有改变局面的能力

V: Carol，我发现原来 Michael 一直在欺骗我！
C: 这个大骗子！那你打算怎么办？
V: 显然是和他分手啊。我还能做什么啊！
C: 没错，骗你第一次就会有第二次！
V: 但我对他还是很有感觉。
C: 你跟他在一起这么长时间了，肯定会有感觉，不过这种感觉会随着时间逐渐冲淡的。
V: 但愿吧。可我还是很想他，怎么办？
C: 我知道！让我们给他点颜色看看！
V: 你是说报复他？怎么做？
C: 没错。你也跟别的男孩交往。
V: 跟谁？
C: 我有一个外校的朋友。帅毙了！我回头给他打个电话，看能不能在周五安排个约会。
V: 周五？可是我们班那天晚上要开晚会啊！
C: 对呀，到时候 Michael 肯定会去的！
V: 就是说，当 Michael 以为我在宿舍哭肿了眼睛的时候，我却与一个大帅哥一同出场，到时候哭的就该是他了！
C: 对啊，这就叫小女子的厉害！

> **Questions 2**
> 1. Have you ever been cheated on by someone? What did you do?
> 2. Do you think it's right to get revenge or should you move on?

Dialogue 3

Sophia: Grace, I need your advice.
Grace: OK. What's your problem?
S: I've been **going out with**[①] Harry ever since high school but now we are studying in different cities and so we hardly communicate anymore.
G: Do you think he still loves you?

S: That's just it! At the beginning of the semester he used to call me every night but now I'm lucky if I get a call once a week!

G: Maybe it's because he's busy with his studies. Do you still love him?

S: I'm not so sure now. There's this cute guy in my class who's always asking me out for dinner.

G: I see. So you have **a new lover on the horizon**②! That's why you're asking me about Harry!

S: Well, yes. So what should I do?

G: Why don't you go out with this new guy and then if you don't like him then you've lost nothing.

S: But if we fall in love then what about Harry?

G: Then **he's history**③! Let's face it. You need someone here and now.

S: But people say that first love never dies!

G: And **the second mouse gets the cheese**④! It's time **to move on**⑤ girl.

Questions 3

① go out with: 男女交往，出去约会
② a new lover on the horizon: 对你一见倾心的人
③ he's history: 属于过去的事情
④ the second mouse gets the cheese: 后来者居上（这是与文化有关的一个俚语。直译是"第二只老鼠有奶酪吃"，因为在英国，人们用逋鼠器抓老鼠时，第一只老鼠显然会被夹住，这样第二只老鼠自然就能顺利地吃到奶酪了。）
⑤ to move on: 忘掉过去，改变方向

S: Grace，你给我些建议吧。

G: 好的，怎么了？

S: 从高中的时候我和 Harry 就开始交往了，可是现在我们在不同的城市上学，我们都没什么可说的了。

G: 你觉得他还爱你吗?

S: 问题就出在这儿！这学期刚开始的时候，他每天晚上都给我打电话。可是现在他一周能给我打一次就算我走运了！

G: 也许是因为他学习太忙吧。你还爱他吗?

S: 我现在不太肯定了。我们班里有一个特别帅的家伙，总是约我出去吃饭。

G: 我明白了。就是说你有新的追求者了。所以你才问我 Harry 的事儿。

S: 是的，我应该怎么办?

G: 你可以和这个家伙约会试一试啊。就算你不喜欢他，你也没有什么损失。

S: 但要是我们相爱了呢？Harry 怎么办?

G: 那他就成为历史了！我们得面对现实！你需要的是一个能够陪伴在你身边的人。

S: 可是人们总是说初恋永远难忘啊。

G: 人们也说后来者居上啊，该换一个了，姐们儿。

Questions 3

1. Who was your first love?
2. Is he still your love or have you moved on?

Love 爱情

Chapter 2   Leisure 休闲时光

5　夜生活
Night Life

Background Information

Night life comprises any form of entertainment that takes place in the evening until the small hours of the next day. It usually means bars, clubs and live entertainment where friends can hang out. Karaoke has been a popular form of entertainment beginning first in Japan, then the rest of East and Southeast Asia, since at least the 1980s. Karaoke machines, which play a background musical track of songs and display their lyrics on a video screen, are found in private karaoke rooms all over China. In March 2006 a curfew was placed on karaoke bars between 2 am and 8 am as a result of the fire on Christmas Day 2005 in Zhongshan, Guangdong Province that killed 26 people.

夜生活是指人们在晚间至第二天凌晨从事的各种形式的娱乐活动，通常就是大家可以聚在一起的酒吧、俱乐部、以及现场娱乐活动。卡拉OK起源于日本，并于20世纪80年代迅速流行至整个东亚及东南亚。在中国的卡拉OK歌房中，一般都有那种用于播放背景音乐、显示歌词的卡拉OK机。2005年圣诞夜，发生在广东省中山市的一场大火夺去了26人的生命，这使得有关部门于2006年3月下发命令，禁止卡拉OK厅在凌晨2点至凌晨8点营业。

背景信息

Dialogue 1

Jim: So, what's happening tonight?

Roy: I don't know, **what do you fancy**?[①]

J: Well, we can go to the Poachers Inn like we usually do. There are always lots of foreigners who go there.

R: That's boring! Same old place, same old faces, same old music. I fancy something new. Let's see what *That's Beijing* says.

J: OK, here it is. Do you want something at the top end, middle of the road or cheap and cheerful?

R: Cheap and cheerful I think. I've got to make my money last until the end of the month.

J: All right. What about the Bus Bar?

R: Never heard of it. What does it say about it?

J: It's two buses gutted out and welded together.

R: Sounds great. What else?

J: The drinks are **dirt cheap**[②]. And it's near the Worker's Stadium so we don't have far to travel.

R: Yeah! Great idea! Let's go and **check it out**[③]! And we can ask Sam to come too; he's always **up for**[④] trying something new!

习惯用语 1

① What do you fancy? 你想做些什么?
② dirt cheap: 很便宜
③ check it out: 调查某件事,去看看什么事
④ up for: 有兴趣做某事

J: 今晚干什么去?
R: 不知道,你有什么好主意吗?

Leisure 休闲时光

J: 那就去我们常去的 Poachers Inn 吧。好多老外都去那里。
R: 太没意思了！老地方，老面孔，老音乐。我想找点儿新鲜的。咱们看看 That's Beijing 上有什么信息。
J: 哦，这儿有。你是想去贵的、一般的，还是既便宜又好玩儿的地方？
R: 我想去既便宜又好玩儿的地方。我这点儿钱得维持到这个月底。
J: 好吧，"公车吧"怎么样？
R: 从没听说过。这报纸上怎么说？
J: 就是把两个公共汽车焊在了一起。
R: 听起来挺不错的。别的呢？
J: 那儿饮料特便宜。而且离工人体育场特近，我们不用走很远。
R: 嗯，好主意！咱们去看看！把 Sam 也叫上，他喜欢尝试新东西！

Questions 1

1. Do you like going to bars? Why? Why not?
2. Have you ever been to a bar where there are mainly foreigners?

Dialogue 2

Maggie: Wow! This is a really cool place! I like the décor.
Audrey: Yeah, I thought you'd like it. The great thing about Latinos is that everyone likes to dance **salsa**[①] here.
M: So I see! I would love to dance like that. It's so sexy.
A: They have free dance classes every night except Monday so you could try it out. Compared to other dances it's relatively easy to learn.
M: How long did it take you to learn?
A: It took about one month to be upgraded from the primary to the secondary class. Now I have learned a lot of new steps.
M: I can't wait to try it! And it's obviously been good for your figure.

A: Yeah. My waist, hips and tummy have all got slimmer.

M: Let's watch some of them dancing and you can tell me what they are doing.

A: Notice that it's always the man who leads and the woman follows.

M: Yeah they seem so enthusiastic about their dancing. It must **burn up a lot of calories**②.

A: Sure does. You need to drink plenty of water.

M: OK. I won't forget. I'll be here tomorrow night for the free class!

习惯用语 2

① salsa: 萨尔萨舞, 一种拉丁舞蹈
② burn up a lot of calories: 燃烧卡路里, 减肥

M: 哇! 这地方太酷了! 我喜欢这里的舞台装饰。
A: 我就知道你会喜欢。拉美人最大的特点就是每个人都喜欢跳萨尔萨舞。
M: 嗯, 看到了! 我也想跳成那样, 简直太性感了!
A: 除了周一, 他们每晚都会举办免费的舞蹈班, 你可以去试试。跟其他舞蹈比起来, 萨尔萨舞算是简单易学的了。
M: 你学了多久?
A: 从初级班到中级班, 我用了大约一个月的时间。现在我已经学了很多新舞步了。
M: 我简直迫不及待了! 显然这对你的体型也很有帮助。
A: 是啊! 我的腰变细了, 屁股和肚子都变小了。
M: 咱们来看看他们跳舞, 你好给我讲解一下动作。
A: 注意, 通常都是由男士领着女士跳。
M: 是啊, 你看他们跳得多有热情啊! 肯定特消耗热量。
A: 那是自然, 你得多喝水。
M: 好的, 记住了。我明晚就来试试免费课程。

> **Questions 2**
> 1. Have you ever tried salsa?
> 2. What's your favourite dance?

Dialogue 3

Vivian: Do you want to go to a karaoke bar tonight? We could get a group together.

Amanda: I'd love to but since the restrictions it means we can't do an **all-nighter**① like we used to and so we have to be back early.

V: I know what you mean. It used to be fun staying up all night. Now we have to leave at 2 am and as the dorms are locked we either have to find a cheap hotel or stay on the streets until 6 am.

A: It's a shame because after a hard week of studying I look forward to an evening of karaoke.

V: Yeah. Karaoke is the best way to relax. There aren't many clubs around, bars are too noisy, and I can't bear cigarette smoke.

A: And it's a cheap form of entertainment!

V: We could always go in the afternoon and that way we could spend a long time there.

A: But it's not the same! I don't see why there's a curfew. After all, we are adults now and can look after ourselves in a responsible way.

V: I agree but the law is the law. There's nothing we can do about that. So what do you think about an afternoon?

A: Who were you thinking of inviting?

V: How about your dorm and mine? That way we could really get

to know one another.
A: Sounds cool. OK, **you're on**②.

> 习惯用语 3
>
> ① all-nighter: 夜不归宿　　② you're on: 成交，就这么定了

V: 你今晚想去唱卡拉 OK 吗？咱们可以一起去。
A: 我想去，可是现在有禁令，我们就不能像过去那样唱整晚了，得早点儿回来。
V: 我明白你的意思。过去唱通宵的时候特别有意思，但现在我们必须在凌晨两点钟的时候离开。而且那个时候宿舍已经关门了，我们得找个便宜的旅馆，要么在大街上闲逛，直到早上 6 点。
A: 真是太讨厌了！辛辛苦苦学了一周，我特想唱一个晚上的卡拉 OK。
V: 没错，唱卡拉 OK 是最好的放松方式。咱们附近没什么俱乐部，酒吧又太吵，而且我受不了酒吧里的烟味。
A: 而且唱卡拉 OK 还很便宜！
V: 咱们可以下午去，那样可以多唱一会儿。
A: 可那感觉就是不一样！我真不明白为什么要有那种禁令。毕竟我们已经是成年人了，可以为自己负责了。
V: 我同意，不过法律毕竟是法律，我们无能为力。所以，咱们下午去怎么样？
A: 你还想叫上谁？
V: 把咱俩的室友都叫上怎么样？那样我们大家都可以认识认识。
A: 好啊，就这么定了！

> Questions 3
>
> 1. Do you like going to karaoke bars?
> 2. When is the best time to go?
> 3. Who do you like to go with?

Chapter 2　Leisure 休闲时光

6　校园里的学生活动
Student Activities on Campus

Background Information

　　There are many activities on campus, such as dancing balls at the weekend and all kinds of organisations set up by students. There would be small parties every week as well as big parties held by the Student Union at graduation time.

　　On average, students participate in 1.8 organisations. According to the Jiangsu Student Federation in 2004 the composition of organisations was

- Freshmen 44%
- Sophomores 30%
- Juniors 18%
- Seniors 7%
- Postgraduates 1%

　　校园里的活动可谓是丰富多样。有周末舞会，有各种学生社团举办的活动。每周有小型聚会，而在毕业的时候学生会还会举办大型晚会。

　　据说每名学生在校期间平均参加1.8个社团组织。根据2004年江苏学生联盟的调查显示，学生社团的成员组成为：

- 一年级新生占44%
- 二年级学生占30%
- 三年级学生占18%
- 四年级学生占7%
- 研究生占1%

背景信息

Dialogue 1

Louise: Cecilia, why aren't you dancing with that boy again? I saw you dance with him twice.
Cecilia: Oh, you know I **can't stand**① him anymore.
L: What's the problem?
C: He kept stepping on my foot. He's really clumsy. I was trying hard not to lose my temper.
L: I see, but he was smiling at you all the time so I guess he likes you.
C: I hope not. How about you? Why are you sitting here all evening?
L: Well, I came with my friend Jenny and you know I don't know how to dance and I always feel embarrassed. When boys come and ask me to dance, I said I can't dance.
C: Come on, everyone has to learn sometime.
L: But if I **make a fool of myself**② then everyone will laugh at me.
C: Of course they won't. It's dark in here, anyway.
L: You're right, but what if my partner laughs at me?
C: I don't think any boy dances very well here so you will probably laugh at him! You know the first time I danced with a boy, he danced worse than me. I asked him, since you can't dance, how dare you invite me to dance?
L: What did he say?
C: He said, because I am sure you dance better than me, so that I want you to teach me.
L: Oh, and what happened then?
C: He's not only my dancing partner but my soul mate too!

习惯用语 1

① can't stand: 无法容忍
② make a fool of oneself: 做傻事, 出洋相

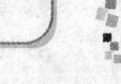

L: Cecilia，你为什么不再跟那个男孩跳舞了？我以前见你跟他跳过两次。
C: 唉，我再也受不了他了！
L: 怎么了？
C: 他老是踩我的脚！笨手笨脚的。我一直在强忍着不发火。
L: 我明白了。可他一直在对你微笑，我猜他喜欢你。
C: 我可不希望。你呢？怎么整晚都坐在这儿？
L: 我跟 Jenny 一起来的，你也知道我不会跳舞，我总是手足无措。男孩们过来邀请我跳舞，我就说我不会跳。
C: 来吧！你迟早总是要学会的。
L: 可要是我出了错，大家都会笑话我的。
C: 肯定不会的，再说这里这么黑，人家也看不见啊。
L: 话是这么说，可要是我的搭档笑话我呢？
C: 我觉得这里的男孩子跳得都不怎么样，你很可能去笑话他们呢！你知道，我第一次跳舞的男舞伴就比我跳得差。我问他，既然你不会，你怎么还敢邀请我跳舞？
L: 他说什么？
C: 他说，因为我确定你跳得比我好啊，所以我想让你教我。
L: 噢，那后来呢？
C: 他不但成了我的舞伴，还成了我的亲密爱人！

Questions 1

1. Did you ever go to dances held in the campus?
2. Are you invited by girls or by boys?

Dialogue 2

Jane: Linda, would you like to go to a painting club with me today? We're learning to draw the human body this evening and one of our students will be picked to be the model.

Linda: That's interesting, but I want to go to the drama society as we will have a role play game this evening.

J: Oh, really? That sounds like fun. What kind of role will you play?

L: That's the problem! I **haven't a clue**①! Our teacher asked us to choose a role which is completely different from our real character. Do you have any suggestions?

J: Let me think. How about a policewoman?

L: No, I can't be so cold and aggressive.

J: You have to try. You are too nice and polite. That role would be totally different from yourself.

L: Well, what other role do you suggest?

J: What about a thief?

L: No, you don't want to ruin my reputation, do you?

J: Of course not. But you are acting, you have to forget who you are and put yourself into your role.

L: Yes, but … what else?

J: Come on, you're too timid. How about a domineering business woman?

L: That's better, but what does a domineering business woman look like?

J: Did you see the movie *The Devil Wears Prada*?

L: Oh yes, it's about a crazy business woman who is very dominating and cruel and demanding.

J: Yes, well then, try to imitate her.

习惯用语 2

① haven't a clue: 不知道怎么办

J: Linda，你今天陪我去写生小组好吗？我们今晚学画人物肖像，其中一个学生将被选为模特。

L: 挺有意思的啊，不过我今晚想去戏剧社，今晚我们有一个角色扮演的游戏。

J: 真的？那肯定特有意思，你扮演什么类型的角色？
L: 问题就在这儿，我还没想好呢。老师要求我们选择一个与真实中的自己完全不同的角色。你有什么建议吗？
J: 我想想啊，你演女警察怎么样？
L: 不行，我可演不了那么酷的角色。
J: 你试一试啊，平时你总是那么彬彬有礼的，这个角色与你本人完全不同。
L: 好吧，你还能想出别的什么角色吗？
J: 要不，演小偷？
L: 不，你也不想毁了我的名声，对吧？
J: 当然不想。不过你是在演戏，你得忘了你是谁，把自己完全融入到角色当中。
L: 是，可是……别的呢？
J: 行了，别犹犹豫豫的。要不演个专横的女强人，怎么样？
L: 这个还好一点儿。可是专横的女强人应该是什么样的呢？
J: 你看过《穿普拉达的女王》那部电影吗？
L: 看过，电影讲的是一位非常独裁、专断、苛刻、疯狂的商界女魔头。
J: 没错。那好，你模仿她试试。

> **Questions 2**
>
> 1. Which clubs or societies have you joined?
> 2. Which do you like best?

Dialogue 3

Sylvia: Are you going to the Christmas Eve party?

Denny: I haven't decided yet. I have an important exam next week, and I haven't prepared for it well.

S: I know you are the top student in our class, but we are humans not machines, we need to relax sometimes.

D: OK, tell me what you guys will do tonight?

S: We will have lots of fun. First, we will have a singing competition.
D: But I can't sing.
S: Doesn't matter. It's just a bit of fun. After that, we will have a game of Touch your Gift.
D: What's Touch your Gift?
S: It's very simple. We will have many boxes and inside each box is a gift. Everyone has a chance to choose one box and feel the gift inside without looking. If you guess what it is, then it's yours. Very simple, right? And we have an Apple iPod as one of the gifts. Do you want a chance to win it?
D: Really? Then I must go to the party.
S: I'm sure you won't regret it. After that, we will go to church to sing **Christmas carols**[①].
D: I've never been inside a church before so that sounds interesting.

习惯用语 3

① Christmas carols: 圣诞颂歌

S: 你打算去参加平安夜晚会吗？
D: 我还没决定呢。我下周有一个很重要的考试还没准备好呢。
S: 我知道你是班里的好学生，可我们是人，不是机器。有些时候我们也需要放松。
D: 好吧，来说说你们都打算在晚会上干什么？
S: 肯定特有趣！首先，我们要赛歌。
D: 可我不会唱歌。
S: 没关系，不过是玩儿玩儿罢了。之后，我们会有一个"摸礼物"的游戏。
D: 什么是"摸礼物"游戏？
S: 很简单，我们把礼物放在不同的盒子里面。每个人都有机会选择一个盒子然后用手摸一摸,但是不能看。你要是猜对了,礼物就归你了。很简单,是吧?礼物中还有 iPod 呢。想不想要?

D: 真的吗?那我绝对去!

S: 我保证你去了不会后悔的,然后我们还会去教堂,唱圣诞歌。

D: 我以前从没进过教堂里边,所以我想去。

Questions 3

1. Do you ever go to parties on campus?
2. What kind of party interests you?

Chapter 2　Leisure 休闲时光

7　音乐与电影
Music and Movies

Background Information

Cinemas are popular in China but relatively expensive considering the ease and cheapness of DVD's. There are more and more multi-screens cinemas.

Motion pictures were introduced to China in 1896, but it was almost a decade before the first local attempt at filmmaking with *Conquering Jun Mountain* (1905). China's first "talkie" was *The Songstress, Red Peony* (1931). Foreign films were first allowed to be shown in 1995. Chinese actors and actresses are starting to appear more regularly in Hollywood films. The Chinese music scene is starting to take off.

电影院在中国很普遍，但是与方便而又价廉的 DVD 相比，看电影则显得有些价格昂贵。现在，出现了越来越多的多影幕电影院。

1896年，电影技术传入中国，但过了将近10年后，中国才于1905年尝试拍摄了第一部电影《定军山》。中国的第一部有声电影是1931年上映的《歌女红牡丹》。外国电影是到1995年才准许在中国上映。中国的男女演员们也开始进军好莱坞，越来越频繁地出现在好莱坞的电影中。中国的音乐市场也在快速发展。

背景信息

Dialogue 1

Kitty: Are you going to Midi?

Beth: Midi? What's that?

K: It's China's largest outdoor music festival. It's held during the May holidays in Haidian Park.

B: I much prefer Western music to Chinese bands so it's **not my kind of scene**①.

K: But that's where you're wrong! Out of 84 bands that will appear this year, 22 of them are foreign.

B: Cool! How much are the tickets?

K: Only 50 yuan for the whole day. That's cheaper than a two-hour concert. And you're not restricted by seats and walls. So you can move around and get as **close to the action**② as you want.

B: You've obviously been before so tell me what it's like.

K: It's a bit wild because everyone's jumping and bumping into each other but it's great fun because everyone's so excited and happy that you just want to do the same.

B: OK I'll go but I've nothing to wear!

K: Wear anything you like. **Anything goes**③. But don't forget it'll be warm so probably the less the better. I'm going to have my hair tinted with blue and yellow streaks. What about you?

B: I'm going to wear some cool **shades**④ and some torn shorts that **show off**⑤ my long legs.

K: Me I'm going for the school look. You know, white shirt and loose tie. I think it really looks sexy.

B: Let's hope the guys think so too. We're going to be two hot super girls!

习惯用语 1

① not sb.'s kind of scene: 不合某人的兴趣（口味、性情等）
② close to the action: 靠近舞台，靠近演出现场
③ anything goes: 一切都许可
④ shades: 太阳镜
⑤ show off: 炫耀

K: 你去"迷笛"吗？

B: "迷笛"？什么东西？

K: 是中国最大的户外音乐节。每年五一长假的时候都会在海淀公园举办。

B: 与中国的那些乐队比起来，我还是更喜欢西方音乐，所以，这个音乐节不符合我的胃口。

K: 那你可错了！今年会有84支乐队登台献艺，其中22支来自国外。

B: 酷！门票多少钱？

K: 才50元，可以玩儿一整天！比两小时一场的音乐会可便宜多了。而且你还不会被座位和围栏束缚着。所以你可以随意移动，靠近那些激动人心的演出现场。

B: 你以前肯定去过，快跟我说说那里怎么样。

K: 感觉有些疯狂，摩肩接踵，不过人们都很兴奋，很有意思，让你也想融入其中。

B: 好吧，我去，可我不知道该穿什么！

K: 喜欢什么就穿什么，什么都行。但是别忘了天气很热，所以还是少穿点为妙。我想把头发染成黄蓝条的。你呢？

B: 我打算戴墨镜，穿撕裂短裤。那样可以秀一下我的长腿。

K: 我打算以学生装束出现。白衬衫，系得松松的领带，我觉得看上去特别性感。

B: 但愿那些男孩子们也这么想。我们会变成两个超级辣妹！

Questions 1

1. Have you ever been to an outdoor music festival?
2. Who's your favourite rock band?

Leisure 休闲时光

Dialogue 2

Kate: Which Chinese actress do you like best?

Tina: I think I'd have to say Gong Li. Ever since she starred in *Red Sorghum* and *Raise the Red Lantern* she's been China's number one.

K: For over twenty years! I much prefer Zhang Ziyi. I thought she was wonderful in *Hero*.

T: She was I agree but in *Memoirs of a Geisha*, although her acting was good, I felt she was **let down**[①] by her poor English. Who do you think's going to be the next Gong Li?

K: Everyone says it must be Zhang Ziyi.

T: Well, I've just seen *Protégé* so I've got to say that it's Zhang Jingchu. And unlike Zhang Ziyi her English is really fluent.

K: Yeah English is **a must**[②] for Chinese actors now as they all seem to end up in Hollywood.

T: That's where Zhang Jingchu made her latest film *Rush Hour 3*. It's **due out**[③] in August.

K: I know very little about her. What other films has she been in?

T: Her first film was *Peacock* in 2005 so she's definitely the rising star of this millennium. All she needs is a male co-star. Wouldn't it be great to have a Chinese couple rival Brad Pitt and Angelina Jolie! Any suggestions?

K: I can't think of anyone Chinese. What about Rain? Now they would make a handsome couple!

T: Yeah. A match made in Hollywood heaven!

K: Now that would definitely be a blockbuster! And who knows, they may even **hit it off**[④] and then we could see the rise of an Asian film dynasty.

T: Yeah. Forget Hollywood. Forget Bollywood. Here comes Chollywood!

> **习惯用语 2**
>
> ① let down: 丢脸，失望
> ② a must: 必不可少的东西
> ③ due out: （电影）按预期上映
> ④ hit it off: 合得来，相处融洽

K: 你最喜欢哪位中国女演员？

T: 巩俐。自从出演《红高粱》和《大红灯笼高高挂》开始，她就奠定了自己中国女一号的地位。

K: 而且一直持续了二十多年！不过，我更喜欢章子怡。我觉得她在《英雄》里的表演简直精彩极了！

T: 没错，我同意。可是在《艺妓回忆录》中，尽管她的表演也十分精彩，但她那糟糕的英语真是令人失望。你觉得谁会成为下一个巩俐？

K: 肯定是章子怡，大家都这么说。

T: 我刚刚看了《门徒》，所以我觉得会是张静初。她的英语相当流利，不像章子怡那样。

K: 没错，对于中国演员来说，他们最终想要闯进好莱坞，英语是必需的。

T: 张静初最近在好莱坞拍摄了《尖峰时刻3》。8月就会公映。

K: 我对张静初了解得很少。她还演过什么别的电影吗？

T: 她的第一部电影是2005年拍摄的《孔雀》，很显然，她是一颗冉冉升起的新星。她需要个男搭档。要是有一对中国搭档可以与布拉德·皮特和安吉丽娜·朱莉相匹敌，那多棒啊！你有什么好的人选吗？

K: 我实在想不出有哪个中国男演员适合。Rain 怎么样？绝对是一对帅气的组合！

T: 嗯，这绝对是"好莱坞造好莱坞设"的一对！

K: 那绝对是一鸣惊人啊！也许他们是绝配，从而让我们看到亚洲电影王朝的兴起呢！

T: 是啊！到时候，什么好莱坞，什么宝莱坞，统统滚蛋，"华莱坞"时代即将来临了！

Questions 2

1. Who's your favourite actress? Why?
2. Which up-and-coming film star do you like?

Dialogue 3

Mandy: Belinda, what do you want to do tonight? We really need to enjoy ourselves and **let our hair down**①.

Belinda: **I couldn't agree with you more.**② I was wondering why not watch a film together?

M: Good idea. Which cinema were you thinking of?

B: None, I've just downloaded a film called *Death Note* and saved it on my computer. So we can watch it in the dorm tonight. I hear it's a popular film on campus these days.

M: Yeah, I heard it's just like the original cartoon. I know it really impressed me. So, I've been looking forward to seeing the film for a long time.

B: So tonight's the night then, Mandy.

M: At last! I've heard that the actor named L is very handsome and cool.

B: Anyway, I think maybe we could buy some snacks to eat and have them while we're watching.

M: Sounds good. It will make our dormitory feel like a real cinema.

B: What a wonderful night we'll have.

M: Let's make it a feast!

习惯用语 3

① let sb.'s hair down: 无拘无束
② I couldn't agree with you more. 我非常赞同。

46

M: Belinda，今晚去干什么？我们太需要放纵一下自己了，得好好享受一下！
B: 我完全赞同！干嘛不一起看场电影，你说呢？
M: 好主意！你想去哪家电影院？
B: 不用，我刚刚下载了一部《死亡笔记》存在电脑里了。我们今晚可以在宿舍里看。我听说最近校园里很流行这部电影。
M: 是的，我听说就跟原版的卡通片一样，我很喜欢，早就想看看电影版的了。
B: 就在今晚看，Mandy。
M: 还有，我听说那个叫 L 的男主角特帅，特酷。
B: 我觉得我们可以买些零食，晚上边看边吃。
M: 听起来不错。这会让我们的宿舍感觉更像真正的电影院。
B: 太棒了！肯定是个美好的夜晚！
M: 这将是一场视觉盛宴！

Questions 3

1. Do you prefer going to the cinema or watching a movie at home?
2. Do you buy DVD's or download movies?

Chapter 2   Leisure 休闲时光

8 保持健康
Keeping Fit

Background Information

According to the latest survey from the State General Sports Administration, about 90 percent of university grads don't do any exercise. In 2005, China had a sporting population of 37 percent. This means that they exercise regularly at least three times a week at a medium-intensity level. Each exercise period should be at least half an hour. By 2010, China wants to raise the figure to 40 percent. Beijing has over 100 health clubs with fees ranging from 1,000 to 6,000 yuan a year.

国家体育总局的一项调查显示,90%的大学生不参加任何体育锻炼。2005年,中国有37%的人口经常参加锻炼,这表明这些人每周至少进行三次中等强度的体育运动,每次运动持续至少半小时。到2010年,中国政府想把这一比例提升至40%。北京拥有100余个健身俱乐部,其年费从1000至6000元不等。

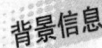

Dialogue 1

Nancy: I took part in an 18-kilometre walk last Sunday but I had to quit after half-an-hour because I was **out of breath**[①]. What can you suggest I do to get fit?

Fitness expert: Try to allocate 20 to 30 minutes for exercise every day.

N: Do I have to join a gym or go to a sports centre?

F: Not at all. You can use any park or grassy area.

N: What kind of exercise should I do?

F: I really recommend jogging because it's easy to do, costs almost nothing and you can do it anywhere and anytime.

N: How fast should I jog?

F: Take it steady[②] at first. After all it's not a race!

N: What should I do if I find it boring?

F: Well, you could find some friends to do it with. Or you could listen to some music on your iPod.

N: Great idea. I'll start tomorrow!

F: That's the way.

习惯用语 1

① out of breath: 上气不接下气   ② take it steady: 缓慢开始

N: 上周日，我参加了一次 18 公里走的活动，可只过了半个小时我就退出了，累得我是上气不接下气。你有什么好的建议能让我身体健康吗？

F: 试一试每天都拿出 20 至 30 分钟来做运动。

N: 我有必要去健身房或体育中心吗？

F: 用不着，在公园里或者草地上就可以。

N: 那我应该做些什么运动呢？

F: 我强烈推荐慢跑。这项运动简单易行，不用什么辅助器械，而且，随时随地都可以进行。
N: 跑多快比较合适？
F: 开始的时候要慢一点。反正又不是赛跑。
N: 要是我觉得无聊怎么办？
F: 那你可以找一些朋友陪你一起运动。或者听听音乐也行。
N: 好主意。我明天就开始！
F: 这就对了，加油！

Questions 1

1. Do you think that you are fit?
2. Do you do any exercise? If so, what kind?

Dialogue 2

Jasmine: Hi Tracey, where are you going?

Tracey: For my weekly **work-out**① at the health club.

J: Do you find that a good way to keep fit?

T: Sure. Haven't you noticed how slim and toned I am?

J: Sorry, I just thought you'd been on a diet.

T: Well a diet helps to lose weight but exercise makes you stronger and really tones the body.

J: Don't you find the exercise a bit boring.

T: Not at all. I spend a little time in the gym but mostly I do aerobic classes. It's great fun and the music is good too.

J: But isn't it expensive?

T: A little but it's worth it for me to keep in shape and you should hear all the **wolf-whistles**② I get in the street!

J: I wish I could go but I don't think I could afford it.

T: Hey, the club's got a special trial discount on at the moment. You could try it for a few sessions and see if you like it.

J: Great! Could you pick up some leaflets for me?
T: Sure thing.

习惯用语 2

① work-out: 锻炼，健身
② wolf-whistles: 男人看到漂亮姑娘时吹的口哨，流氓哨

J: 你去哪儿，Tracey?
T: 去健身俱乐部锻炼。
J: 那对保持体形有帮助吗?
T: 当然了，你没发现我现在的身材苗条而又强健吗?
J: 不好意思，我还以为你一直在节食呢。
T: 节食只是降低体重，但锻炼却能使你变得更强壮，而且对身体确实大有好处。
J: 你不觉得那种锻炼有点儿无聊吗?
T: 没有啊。我练器械的时间很短，大部分时间都去做有氧操课，特有意思，而且背景音乐也很棒。
J: 是不是特贵啊?
T: 有一点儿，不过能够保持体形，我觉得还是值得的。而且走在大街上还经常有帅哥对我吹口哨!
J: 我也想去，可我没那么多钱。
T: 最近俱乐部正在做一次体验的折扣活动。你可以试试，看看自己是否感兴趣。
J: 太好了! 你帮我拿些宣传单好吗?
T: 没问题!

Questions 2

1. Have you ever been to a health club?
2. Would you like to work-out once or twice a week?

Dialogue 3

Shane: Hi Alex. I'm glad I **caught you**[①]. It's about the football team.

Alex: I know what you're going to say. You want to know why the coach **dropped you**[②].

S: Yeah. I was the leading scorer last year. How can he do this to me?

A: Simple. You're not fit enough to play. Since you came back after Spring Festival you're not the player you used to be. What happened?

S: Well, I admit I ate a lot and maybe **put on**[③] a few pounds.

A: A few pounds! It looks like there's two of you!

S: Ha ha. OK I'd better start losing weight.

A: Let's set up a fitness programme. We need you to do some extra training and to watch your food intake.

S: How long will it take?

A: At least a month to get you back to what you were.

S: A month! What will the team do without me?

A: We'll try not to lose too many matches but maybe in a couple of weeks we can put you on the bench.

S: The bench! I've never been a substitute before! How can I **live down**[④] the shame?

A: By scoring as many goals as you can!

习惯用语 3

① catch sb.：遇到某人
② drop sb.：把某人除名
③ put on：增加（体重）
④ live down：通过行动使人原谅

S: 很高兴见到你，Alex。我想跟你说说足球队的事。
A: 我知道你要说什么，你想问，为什么教练不要你了，对吧？

S: 是的。我是去年的主要得分手，你们怎么能这么对我？
A: 很简单，因为你的体形已经不适合运动了。自从你春节回来后就像变了个人似的。怎么了你？
S: 好吧，我承认我吃了很多，长了几斤肉。
A: 几斤？！你简直增加了一倍！
S: 哈哈！好吧，我开始减肥。
A: 那咱们制定一个减肥计划吧。我们需要你多做运动，而且严格控制进食量。
S: 要持续多久啊？
A: 要想让你恢复原来的状态，至少得一个月。
S: 一个月！球队没了我怎么成？
A: 我们尽量少输球，但也许两周后，我们会让你做替补队员。
S: 替补！我从没当过替补！我怎么能承受这种羞辱！？
A: 那你就靠多进球雪耻啊！

Questions 3

1. Are you fit enough to play for your team?
2. What kind of things would you include in a fitness programme?

Leisure 休闲时光

53

Chapter 3　Shopping 购物

9　服装
Clothes

Background Information

The kind of clothes you wear are a fashion statement and also a statement of who you are. They allow you the opportunity to express your taste and individuality at the same time. The following are some common styles found on campus:

Punk: loud rebellious look, studded bag/belt, black skinny pants, fishnet stockings, sneakers, well-worn leather or faded jean jacket.

Preppy: scholarly look, button-down shirt, sweater, khaki pants, blue blazer, loafers, pleated skirt.

Skater: easygoing sporty look, T-shirt, hooded sweatshirt, pants in navy, khaki, or black sneakers and a Beanie cap.

穿在你身上的服装是一种对时尚与自我的传递，你可以借此表达你的品位，宣扬你的个性。下面是一些在校园里常见的服装风格：
- 朋克风格：

张扬、叛逆的风格：有装饰钉的背包或皮带，黑色紧身瘦腿裤子，网眼长袜，运动鞋，穿旧了的皮夹克或褪色的牛仔夹克。
- 学院风格：

一副学生打扮：衬衫的衣扣一扣到底，针织衫，卡其布的裤子，蓝色运动夹克，平底船鞋，褶裙。
- 嘻哈风格：

一身宽松、运动的装扮：T恤衫，帽衫，海军蓝或者卡其色裤子，脚穿黑色运动鞋，头戴一顶无檐小便帽。

背景信息

Dialogue 1

Jenny: Wow, Susie, I really like what you're wearing.
Susie: Thanks, Jenny. It's the Boho look.
J: The Bo what?
S: Boho. It's short for Bohemian. It's a kind of gypsy look with long colourful dresses, plenty of jewelry and scarves.
J: Well, it certainly suits you but I prefer a T-shirt and jeans any day.
S: You have the figure for it and in those **figure-hugging**① jeans and tight T-shirt you look really sexy. But I prefer a more feminine look and it's so cool to wear during summer.
J: What do you mean by feminine? I think I look very feminine!
S: You do but your clothes leave very little to the imagination whereas mine conceals but yet tantalises at the same time.
J: Clever thinking! But I like to let boys know what they're missing!
S: Yeah, well you look really **hot**② in those clothes!
J: Thanks. Why don't we **go for a stroll**③ around the campus and see if we can **raise the boy's temperatures**④ a little!
S: Yeah! Let's go for a stroll and roll our you know what's!

习惯用语 1

① figure-hugging: 包身的衣服，能够展示女性身材的紧身衣服
② hot: 性感的
③ go for a stroll: 漫步
④ raise sb.'s temperatures: 让某人热血沸腾

J: 哇，Susie，你今天的衣服可真漂亮，我很喜欢。
S: 谢谢，Jenny。这是波希米亚风格的着装。
J: 波什么？
S: 波希米亚风格。就是那种身穿彩色长裙，佩戴丝巾还有好多珠宝

的吉普赛着装风格。

J: 嗯，这倒很配你，不过我还是更喜欢T恤和牛仔裤。

S: 你身材好，再穿上紧身的仔裤和T恤，就更性感了。我倒是更喜欢女性化的着装，而且夏天穿起来也很凉快。

J: 你说的女性化是什么意思？我觉得我看上去很女性化！

S: 你是很女人，可你的着装却不是。你穿的衣服过于显露身材，所以反倒不能给人很多想象的空间，而我的衣服能做到藏而不露，但却能让人产生联想。

J: 鬼主意还真不少。但我喜欢直截了当，让男孩子们大饱眼福，看到我的身材。

S: 是的，你穿那些衣服看上去性感极了！

J: 谢谢。咱们到校园里逛逛吧，看能不能吸引一下男生的眼球！

S: 好！咱们去逛逛，展示一下自己，你明白我的意思了！

Questions 1

1. What kind of clothes do you like to wear?
2. Do you like to wear sexy clothes?
3. Do you like to dress for yourself or for the opposite sex?

Dialogue 2

David: Hi Karl. You're looking a bit **down in the mouth**①. What's up?

Karl: And down in the pocket too! It's my girlfriend Nancy. She's always dragging me around shopping with her. And she expects me to pay for everything!

D: What a **bummer**②, man! Still, it's expected, you know.

K: I know, but I really hate spending hours in a clothes shop while she tries on everything in the store! It's so boring!

D: For you, yes but girls like to do that. Just like we can spend hours watching football or basketball. I guess our brains are just wired differently.

K: Suppose so, I guess. It's just that it's costing me a fortune!

D: You should see it as an investment. And of course, if you keep her happy then she should keep you happy too, you know what I mean?

K: She does look after me well. She's always buying me fruit and things like that.

D: That's good. So she cares about your health while spending your wealth!

K: That's one way of putting it. I guess we're happy enough together. That's the main thing.

D: Do you want to go for a beer?

K: I'd love to but I can't afford it!

习惯用语 2

① down in the mouth: 沮丧，垂头丧气
② bummer: 令人不愉快的事（或经历）

D: Karl，你怎么垂头丧气的，怎么了？

K: 我的钱包更是"垂头丧气"！都怪我女朋友 Nancy。她总是拉着我陪她逛商场，还老想让我给她买单！

D: 你可真是个倒霉蛋！不过这也在情理之中，你知道的。

K: 我知道，可她在店里试这试那，我一等就是好几个小时！无聊透了！

D: 那是你觉得无聊，女孩子们可是乐此不疲啊！就跟我们花好几个小时看足球或篮球赛一样。我估计男女大脑的构造就是不同。

K: 也许是吧。关键是我老得花钱啊！

D: 你得把这看作是一项投资。当然，你让她快乐，她就让你快乐，你明白我的意思吧？

K: 她倒是对我挺好的。老是给我买水果什么的。

D: 这不是挺好嘛。她在花你的钱财，同时也关注你的健康。

K: 这倒是，我觉得我们在一起挺快乐的，这是最主要的。

D: 去喝杯啤酒怎么样？

K: 我倒是想去，可我没钱啊！

> **Questions 2**
> 1. Does your boyfriend go shopping with you?
> 2. Do you think it's right for the boy to pay for everything?
> 3. Do you buy him anything?

Dialogue 3

Tom: Oh! Mike, you have so many fashionable clothes!

Mike: Thank you. But only some of them are the ones I really like.

T: So why buy them if you don't like them?

M: Because they make me look cool! And you know how the girls love cool guys!

T: Yeah, I know and that's why I don't have a girlfriend! My clothes are just so ordinary.

M: If you took a bit more of an interest in clothes than in playing computer games you'd soon be **scoring**① with the girls.

T: Yeah, but I just don't have any **dress sense**②. And besides, I prefer to wear comfortable clothes like this football shirt.

M: Well, football shirts are alright for playing football but if you want to really impress the girls then you've got to get some designer clothes.

T: But doesn't it cost a lot of money?

M: Not if you know where to go! You should come with me sometime.

T: Yes. I'd love to.

M: But you can't come with me dressed like that! Have a look in my wardrobe and see if there's anything you like.

T: Oh! This blue T-shirt looks so snazzy.

M: If you like it, I will be happy to give it to you as a present.

T: Thanks! So, I'll be able to look cool now!
M: We'll go to Xidan this weekend and I can show you the shops and what's new.

习惯用语 3

① score: 成功，走运
② dress sense: 具有正确的穿着搭配品位

T: 哦！Mike，你的时髦衣服可真不少啊！
M: 谢谢啊！不过我只喜欢其中的一部分。
T: 你不喜欢干嘛还买呀？
M: 因为穿起来很酷啊！你知道那些女孩子就喜欢酷哥。
T: 我知道，这就是我找不到女朋友的原因！我的衣服太一般了。
M: 要是你对着装的兴趣大于对电脑游戏的兴趣，那你早就搞到女朋友了！
T: 嗯，可我就是没有什么穿衣品位！而且，我喜欢穿舒服的衣服，比如这件足球衫。
M: 踢球的时候穿足球衫还差不多，但你要是真的想让那些女孩子对你有印象，你还是得买些品牌服装。
T: 但那不是很贵吗？
M: 找对地方就不贵！没事儿的时候多跟我去逛逛。
T: 嗯，我倒是愿意去。
M: 但你可别穿成这样跟我一起出门啊！去我的衣柜挑挑，看有没有你喜欢的。
T: 哦！这件蓝T恤看上去挺时髦的。
M: 你要是喜欢就送你做礼物吧。
T: 谢谢！我现在看起来够酷吧？
M: 这周末咱俩去西单，我带你去转转，看看有什么新货。

Questions 3

1. Are you interested in the latest fashions?
2. What kind of clothes do you usually wear?

Chapter 3　Shopping 购物

10　购物广场与超市
Malls and Supermarkets

Background Information

　　Malls are becoming very popular in China. By 2010 China is expected to be home to at least seven of the world's 10 biggest shopping centres. Many new malls being built at the moment are trying to be different. The Place in Beijing is 80,000 square metres with a 250 metre-long, 30 metre-wide skyscreen suspended six-stories high. The D·PARK fashion club is in an old electrical factory and incorporates huge gas tanks, big blast furnaces and boilers as part of its fashionable décor. Big supermarket chains like Carrefour and Wal-Mart are set to expand rapidly throughout China.

　　大型购物广场在中国日渐流行。预计到 2010 年，世界十大购物中心至少有七个将陆续落户中国。许多目前在建的购物广场都力求与众不同。北京的世贸天阶购物中心建筑面积达 8 万平方米，拥有一个 250 米长、30 米宽的大屏幕，悬挂在六层楼高的地方。D·PARK 时尚会所则是在一个废旧的电厂里，里面有大型的煤气罐、鼓风炉、锅炉等作为其时尚的装饰。大型的连锁超市，比如家乐福、沃尔玛也正在中国迅速扩张。

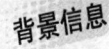

Dialogue 1

Janet: Hi there. Could I have some coleslaw please?
Delicatessen assistant: How much would you like?
J: Just a hundred grams, please.
D: OK. Anything else?
J: Yeah some corned beef, about 200 grams, erm … some green olives, a hundred grams or so, and some cheddar cheese, about 500 grams worth.
D: OK, no problem.
J: I'm having a party so I thought I'd **throw a buffet**①. Any suggestions?
D: Well, you should have a selection of **cold cuts**② and I'd really suggest some of our salads.
J: OK. Can you choose some for me?
D: We also have a special offer today on salami, it's half price. Can I tempt you?
J: Go on then! Give me a hundred grams of that too.
D: Here you are. Is that everything?
J: That's everything. Thanks very much.

习惯用语 1

① throw a buffet: 提供自助餐，提供冷肉、沙拉、三明治等多种选择
② cold cuts: 熟食冷拼盘

J: 你好，我想要点儿凉拌卷心菜，好吗？
D: 要多少？
J: 100 克就够了。
D: 好，别的还要什么？
J: 腌牛肉 200 克，嗯……绿橄榄 100 克左右还有切达干酪，大概 500 克吧。

D: 好的，没问题。
J: 我打算办个晚会，会提供自助餐。你有什么好建议吗？
D: 嗯，那你得多准备点熟食冷盘，而且我强烈建议你买点儿我们店里的沙拉。
J: 好，你帮我选点儿好吗？
D: 我们今天的意大利腊肠也是特供的，半价！有兴趣吗？
J: 好啊！给我来 100 克！
D: 给你。还要别的吗？
J: 不用了，非常感谢！

Questions 1

1. Do you buy most of your food from a supermarket?
2. What are the advantages of shopping in a supermarket?

Dialogue 2

Cynthia: You know the management of the supermarket in our campus is pretty bad.

Natalie: Oh, why do you say that?

C: There are only two assistants at the check-out. You know at peak times, there is always a long line of people waiting to be served.

N: I know, sometimes it's the same in my campus too. I just avoid going there then.

C: I really don't know why they can't arrange more people to work there at noon and dinner time.

N: What really **bugs me**[①] is that they have several assistants just standing there doing nothing! Why can't they be gainfully employed!

C: I think they are just on the look-out for shoplifters so that's their job. They might look as if they are not doing anything but they are!

N: Well I still think they should employ more staff then or they will lose customers!
C: Well, I think maybe it's difficult to do that, if more people are working at noon and in the evening, what would they do the rest of the time? Plus the profit for a small supermarket is very little, so if they did that they might have to raise prices.
N: Sounds reasonable. Anyway, the food is fresh and the ladies are friendly there, so we can't really complain.
C: That's right and it really makes our lives more convenient.

习惯用语 2

① bug sb.: 困扰某人

C: 你知道嘛，我们学校里那家超市的管理特差劲。
N: 为什么那么说?
C: 出口收银处只有两名店员。在高峰的时候有一大堆排大队等着交钱的人。
N: 我知道，我们学校那家有时候也这样。我都避免高峰时期去买东西。
C: 我就不明白他们为什么不能在中午和晚上多安排一些工作人员。
N: 更令我郁闷的是，有些员工就站在那里什么也不干! 完全像废物一样!
C: 我估计他们是在巡视，防止小偷，这就是他们的工作。他们假装看上去无所事事，其实是在工作!
N: 嗯，我还是觉得他们应该多雇点儿人，不然顾客会流失的!
C: 我觉得这有点儿难办，要是为了中午和晚上就多雇人，那其他时间他们干什么呢? 而且小超市的利润是很低的，他们要是多雇人，就得提高商品的价格。
N: 听上去挺有道理。不管怎么说，那里的东西都挺新鲜，服务员态度也很好，我们也没什么太多可抱怨的。
C: 没错，而且它真的为我们的生活提供了便利。

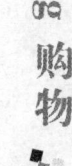

Questions 2

1. Do you shop in the supermarket on campus or do you shop in other places?
2. What do you think of the service in the supermarket in your campus?

Dialogue 3

Bill: Hey Thomas, are you free this afternoon?
Thomas: Yes, why?
B: I want to buy a pair of Nike shoes. Can you go to The Place with me?
T: That's the new mall in the CBD. It's supposed to have the biggest LED screen in Asia. It's 250 metres long! Why not! I've been thinking of buying a Li Ning jacket too.
B: Great, hurry up.
(In the mall)
B: This pair is so cool. I've seen Kobe Bryant wearing similar ones on TV before. What do you think?
T: It's nice, how much is it?
B: Here's the price, 800 RMB.
T: Don't you think it's too much for shoes?
B: No, these are not just shoes but a life style! They say that the guy who wears these is **cool, hip and with it**[①]. You like Li Ning because you like its image. I think Nike's image is more international and cool.
T: But last month I saw some Nike shoes in the street market and they only cost one hundred.
B: That's because they're not original ones, they're copies. I don't want cheap copies, I want the real thing.
T: OK, I hope you won't regret buying them when you have no money to have dinner.

B: Come on buddy, we are best friends aren't we?
T: Yes, but I'm not going to lend you any money!

习惯用语 3

① cool, hip and with it: 时髦的，流行的

B: Thomas，你今天下午有空吗？
T: 有，怎么了？
B: 我想买双"耐克"鞋。你陪我去趟"世贸天阶"好吗？
T: 就是那个在CBD新开的购物广场吧。拥有全亚洲最大的LED屏幕，有250米长呢！干嘛不去啊！我也想买一件"李宁"的夹克呢。
B: 好极了！走吧！
(在商场里)
B: 这双鞋真酷啊。我以前在电视上看到Kobe Bryant穿过一双跟这个差不多的。你觉得怎么样？
T: 挺好看的，多少钱？
B: 800块。
T: 你不觉得一双鞋800块钱，太贵了吗？
B: 不，这不仅仅是一双鞋，更是一种生活方式！人们都说穿这双鞋的人很时尚。你喜欢"李宁"，是因为你喜欢它的形象。我觉得"耐克"的形象更国际化，更酷！
T: 可我上个月在街边市场看见卖"耐克"鞋了，也就100块钱。
B: 因为那不是真的，是仿的。我不想买便宜的假货，我想买真品。
T: 好吧，到时候你没钱吃饭，可别后悔买这双鞋。
B: 别呀兄弟，咱们是好朋友，不是吗？
T: 是，可我不打算借给你钱！

Questions 3

1. Do you often shop in a mall?
2. Do you think the products sold in a mall are all original?

Chapter 3 Shopping 购物

11 街边市场
Street Markets

Background Information

　　Street markets are where people sell small stuff on both sides of a certain street, the products are books, cosmetics, all kinds of dresses, trinkets, etc. They are certainly cheaper than in the malls but without any guarantee of the quality. It is more popular in the evening than in the day time.

　　In Beijing there is the Donghuamen Night Market which is just next to Wangfujing. Here you can find just about anything on a stick from insects, worms to seahorses.

　　街边市场就是指那些在马路边上供人们兜售小物件的市场，所售商品有书籍、化妆品、服装、小饰品等等。与大商场里的东西相比，自然是比较便宜，但是却没有任何质量保证。这种市场多出现于傍晚时分，白天则比较少见。

　　在北京，有个东华门夜市就在王府井附近，那里卖的小吃从小昆虫到海马，卖什么的都有。

背景信息

Dialogue 1

Vera: Would you like to go to the street market with me after dinner?
Lena: I went there last week.
V: Oh, did you buy anything?
L: Well, I bought a handbag. And I think I will not buy them from there anymore.
V: Why, what happened?
L: I found there was a hole inside after I got home.
V: You should have checked it carefully before you bought it.
L: Yes, but I was in a hurry and I even didn't bargain with the lady for as long as I usually do.
V: See, that's why you got a **crappy** [1] handbag. In fact, you can find some good and cheap things in the street market if you browse carefully.
L: So you seem to be an expert on street market shopping then.
V: Well, maybe.
L: Then share with me your experience.
V: Well, first of all, you shouldn't show you are interested even if you really like that product. When you find something you like, you should just ask the price and try to leave. Then the seller will try to keep you by lowering the price.
L: How about if he or she lets me go?
V: Then you go and look for the same thing in the next stall.
L: OK, if they ask me to stay, what should I say next?
V: Then you begin to bargain with them, as low as possible, until you have an agreement on the price.
L: Then?
V: Then you can check the product carefully. See if there is any problem or if it is a used one. Only when you find everything is OK, should you pay and take the goods.

习惯用语 1

① crappy: 质量不好的，蹩脚的

V: 吃完晚饭，咱们一起去路边的那个市场逛逛怎么样？
L: 我上礼拜刚去过。
V: 买什么东西了没有？
L: 买了个手提包。我想我再也不会从那儿买东西了。
V: 为什么啊？
L: 我到家后发现包上有一个洞。
V: 那你买之前应该好好检查一下。
L: 是，可我当时着急啊，我都没怎么跟那个卖东西的小姐砍价，要是在平时我会和他们砍价的。
V: 你瞧，难怪你买回这个破烂东西啊。其实只要你肯下功夫仔细逛，在那个路边市场里还是能找到一些又好又便宜的东西的。
L: 听你这意思，你好像是个街边市场购物专家啊。
V: 还真没准。
L: 那跟我分享一下你的经验吧。
V: 首先，即便你真的很喜欢某样东西，也不能让人觉得你对它感兴趣。发现了喜欢的，就问问价格，然后离开。到时候卖主自然就会压低价格留住你了。
L: 那他/她要是不理我呢？
V: 那你就走啊，到别的摊儿上再找找同样的东西。
L: 好，要是他们让我留下，我应该说什么？
V: 那你就开始讨价还价，尽可能地压低价格，直到你满意为止。
L: 然后呢？
V: 然后你就仔细检查一下商品。看看有没有问题，是不是被人用过。要是什么问题都没有，你就可以付钱买了。

Questions 1

1. Do you ever shop in street markets?
2. Do you like or dislike street markets? Why?

Dialogue 2

Laura: Why are you so late back? You look so tired. What have you been doing?

Natalie: I caught a thief.

L: Oh, congratulations! But what happened?

N: I went to the street market with Kitty today. I bought some T-shirts and she was going to buy some books. Then we went to a book stall and **had a browse**①, but she didn't find any books that interested her. So we left and went to the bus station. Then I couldn't find my purse which has my bus IC card inside.

L: Oh, that's awful.

N: Yes, so I tried to remember when I had it last. Before I went to the book stall, my purse was still there. And when we were looking at books, both of us bent down, and I put my bag on my back.

L: I guess someone stole it then.

N: Yes, so I went back to the book stall and asked the seller if she saw anyone behind me when I was looking at the books. She said, she saw a boy behind me and thought that was my friend. And she described his features to me.

L: So what happened next?

N: We were sure the boy was still somewhere close. Since he managed to steal my purse he would probably try for another one too. So we wandered about and looked for him. And finally I saw him nearby.

L: So you **grabbed hold of**② him?

N: No, he looked too strong for me. Luckily there was a policeman so I told him what had happened. He watched him for a while and when he attempted to open an old lady's bag

the policeman arrested him.

L: You are so brave. So did you get your purse back?

N: No, but I got back my money. The thief took the money out and threw my purse into a rubbish bin.

L: Well, that's not too bad and you helped a policeman to catch a thief. That really impresses me.

习惯用语 2

① have a browse: 随便看看
② grab hold of: 抓住

L: 你怎么回来这么晚？还特疲惫的。干嘛去了你？

N: 我抓了一个小偷。

L: 哦！恭喜啊！怎么回事儿？

N: 今天我和 Kitty 一起去街边市场。我买了几件 T 恤，她想买些书。然后我们就去书店随便逛逛，但并没有发现她感兴趣的书。于是我们就走了，去车站等车。但我却找不到我的钱包，我的公交 IC 卡就放在里面了。

L: 天哪！太遭糕了！

N: 是啊，所以我就努力回忆最后一次拿钱包是在哪里。我去书店之前，钱包还在呢。后来我们看书的时候，都特专注，我就把书包背在后面了。

L: 我估计就是那时候被偷走的。

N: 嗯，因此我又回到书店，问售货员我在看书的时候，看没看见有人在我身后。她说看见一个男孩在我身后，还以为是我朋友呢。然后就跟我描述了一下那个人的样子。

L: 后来呢？

N: 我们确定那个男孩没有走远。因为他既然偷了我的钱包，就还会再偷别人的。我们就四处找，发现他就在附近。

L: 然后你就抓住他了？

N: 没有，他可比我壮多了。好在那里有一个警察，我就把事情的来龙去脉都告诉了他。他一直监视着那个小偷，就在那个小偷想要再次对一个老太太下手的时候，警察上去抓住了他！

L: 你太勇敢了！钱包拿回来了吗？

N: 没有，不过钱倒是拿回来了。那个小偷把钱拿出来后就把我的钱包扔进垃圾箱了。

L: 哦，好在钱拿回来了，还不至于那么糟。你帮警察抓小偷，真让我佩服！

Questions 2

1. Did you have any good or bad experience when shopping in a street market?
2. What do you think of that?

Dialogue 3

Jason: Oh, my girlfriend's birthday is coming, what should I give her as a gift?

Dylan: Well, you can go to the street market and have a look.

J: Are you kidding me?① If she knows the gift was bought in a street market she will say goodbye to me for sure.

D: But she won't know if you don't tell her. Most goods there are similar to those in the mall and some are the same I think. What's more, love is priceless.

J: I still think it's not right. You know I love her very much.

D: Yes, I know that. But we are students. I don't think we should spend lots of money on luxury gifts we can't afford. You can buy a stone necklace in the street market for her now and buy a real diamond necklace in a jewellery shop one day in the future.

J: If she **dumps**② me when I give her the stone necklace then what do I do?

D: Then let her go. It proves she doesn't really love you.
J: Oh, no, I don't want her to leave me.
D: Don't worry, I'm sure she won't. She is not that superficial. I'm sure she loves you more than an expensive gift.
J: Yes, I agree with you, that's why I love her very much.

习惯用语 3

① Are you kidding me? 你在开玩笑吗?
② dump: 分手, 甩掉

J: 我女朋友的生日就快到了，我该送她什么作礼物呢?
D: 你可以去路边那个市场转转。
J: 你开玩笑呢吧? 要是她知道礼物是从路边市场买的，肯定跟我分手。
D: 但你要是不告诉她，她也不知道啊。那里的好多东西都跟大商场里的差不多，我觉得有的就完全一样。更重要的是，爱是无法用价钱来衡量的。
J: 我还是觉得不太对。你知道我很爱她。
D: 是，我知道。可我们还是学生啊。我觉得我们不应该花很多钱去买那些我们根本买不起的奢侈礼物。你可以在路边市场给她买一条石头项链，等将来有钱了，再到珠宝店给她买真正的钻石项链。
J: 要是我送她一条石头项链，她要跟我掰了怎么办?
D: 那就随她去吧。这说明她并不是真的爱你。
J: 不, 我不想让她离开我。
D: 别着急，我保证她不会离开你的。她没那么肤浅。我确信她更爱的是你，而不是昂贵的礼物。
J: 嗯, 你说得没错，这就是我深爱她的原因。

Questions 3

1. Do you ever buy gifts for your friends from the street market?
2. Would you be glad to receive a gift from the street market?

Chapter 3 Shopping 购物

12 网上购物
Online Shopping

Background Information

Online shopping is becoming more and more popular in China. It either takes the form of B2C (business to customer) or C2C (customer to customer). The two major reasons why growth is slow are first, concerns about security and reliability and second, Chinese customers are used to haggling over prices in stores, a process which does not transfer to the Internet. According to a China Internet Network Information Centre report of June 2006, the number of online C2C shoppers was 2 million in the cities of Beijing, Shanghai and Guangzhou. The overall figure for China's shoppers, according to CRI English online, is that 31 million people shop online and spent an average of 563 yuan in 2006. Mobile phones, digital products, cosmetics and laptops are the most popular products.

网上购物在中国正日渐流行。采取的形式为B2C（商家对顾客）或者C2C（顾客对顾客）。导致网上购物发展缓慢的原因有两个：首先，是安全与可靠性的问题；其次，中国的顾客都喜欢在商场里讨价还价，但在网上却没有这个过程。2006年6月，中国互联网信息中心的报告显示，在北京、上海和广州这样的大城市，在线C2C的购物者有200万人。而中国国际广播电台"英文在线"节目的数据显示，2006年中国的网上购物人数为3100万，人均消费为563元。手机、数码产品、化妆品、笔记本电脑是网上购物者最常购买的物品。

背景信息

Dialogue 1

Sophia: Wow, where did you get all these amazing new clothes?
Cherry: Online, of course. It's the new convenient way of shopping. No more queuing or haggling with shop assistants!
S: But isn't it risky?
C: Only if you're inexperienced and don't **know the ropes**①. You need to choose an agent with high credibility and follow auction rules.
S: So how do I start online shopping?
C: Have a look at Taobao. com and see what it's like. It's one of the biggest auction websites with about 30 million yuan's worth of transactions every day.
S: Wow! That's a lot. So what have you bought from them recently?
C: Well, I really like Jennifer Lopez perfume and I can get a 30 ml bottle for 100 yuan compared to 340 yuan in Beijing.
S: That's a bargain!
C: Well you need to **shop around**② first. Some agents buy something through another online agents and then sell it at a much higher price so you need to do some market research first before you commit yourself.
S: Why don't we look together at the website first and then you can show me what to do?
C: OK, no problem. It's easy to register on Taobao.
S: Let's go then!

习惯用语 1

① know the ropes: 熟悉内幕，懂得秘诀
② shop around: 货比三家，（在购物之前）对商店逐个进行比较

S: 哇哦！你这些漂亮衣服都是在哪儿买的啊？
C: 当然是在网上了。这可是新式的便捷购物方式。不用排队，也不用与店员讨价还价。
S: 可是不会有什么风险吗？
C: 要是你没什么经验而且不懂其中道道的话，就会有风险。你得选择一个信誉高的网上店铺，而且要严格执行相应的拍卖规则。
S: 我该如何开始网上购物呢？
C: 先去"淘宝"随便看看，了解一下网上购物是怎么回事儿。这是一个日交易额超过3000万元的拍卖网站。
S: 天哪！那么多。你最近从网上买什么了？
C: 我特喜欢 Jennifer Lopez 的香水，30ml 只卖 100 块钱，要在北京买，得 340 块钱呢。
S: 那么便宜！
C: 不过首先你得货比三家，逐店比较一下。有的店铺就是从别的店铺买东西，然后再以更高的价格出售，所以在你决定买东西之前，首先要做一下市场调查。
S: 咱们一起在网上看看吧，你好教教我怎么做，好吗？
C: 好的，没问题。在"淘宝"注册很简单的。
S: 我们现在就上网看看吧。

Questions 1

1. Have you ever done any online shopping?
2. Do you know anybody who does?

Dialogue 2

Brenda: This Yonex racquet is better than the last one you had. Did you buy another one?
Sonya: No, the guy **changed it**[①] for me.
B: Which guy?
S: Well, I bought the last one from a guy online. And it broke after I used it a few times. Then, I contacted that guy and he

agreed to exchange it for me, so this is the replacement.

B: Oh, I see. I never buy anything online; I don't want to be **ripped off**[②].

S: Yes, shopping online does have more risks, but it's not as dangerous as you think. I talked to that guy a few times and got to know that he's a racquet collector and he has an expert knowledge about badminton and racquets. That's why I bought from him.

B: But why did he give you a faulty one at first?

S: He didn't know it himself. That racquet was an old one which was produced many years ago and he had had it for several years too. He showed me it on webcam and as I liked that style, so I bought it. It was maybe harmed by the humidity. That's why it broke.

B: I see, was he polite when you wanted to change it?

S: He was, and he kept on asking me whether I liked it after I bought it.

B: That means he didn't have the intention to con you.

S: Right. He was very apologetic when I told him it was broken, and he insisted on changing a new one for me immediately.

B: He is a good online seller.

S: Yes, I hope all the online sellers are like him.

习惯用语 2

① chang it: 兑换，交换，更换　　② rip off: 被宰，受骗

B: 这个 Yonex 的球拍可比你原来那个好多了。是新买的吗？

S: 不是，那个家伙给我换了。

B: 哪个家伙？

S: 我上次那个球拍是在网上的一个人那里买的。没用几次就坏了。

后来我与卖家联系，他同意给我更换。这就是那个新换来的。
B: 哦，明白了。我从不在网上买东西，不想被骗。
S: 是的，网上购物的风险确实比较高，但也没你想得那么危险。我跟那个卖家聊过几次，知道他收集球拍，了解很多关于羽毛球和球拍的知识。所以我才从他那里买东西。
B: 那他一开始为什么给你一个次品啊？
S: 他自己也不知道。那个球拍是好几年前生产的了，而且在他那里也放了好几年了。他通过网络视频向我展示了那个球拍，我很喜欢，然后就买了。估计是时间太长，受潮了，所以就坏了。
B: 哦，那你想换东西的时候，他态度很礼貌吗？
S: 态度非常好，而且一直问我买了以后是不是喜欢。
B: 就是说，他并不想抵赖。
S: 没错。我跟他说球拍坏了的时候，他非常愧疚，而且坚持要给我立刻换个新的。
B: 真是个好卖家啊。
S: 是啊，我希望所有的网上卖家都能像他一样。

Questions 2

1. Do you have any good or bad experiences on shopping online?
2. What would you do if you bought something faulty?

Dialogue 3

Max: How is your online jeans business these days?
Cathy: Well, not as good as at the beginning.
M: Oh, why? They were **selling like hot cakes**[①] last year.
C: Yes, they were. But now, my friend who was working in that factory which provided me with jeans is not working there anymore, and the factory refused to give me a low price and the delivery is always very late.
M: I see, was your friend the factory manager?
C: No, but he was in charge of the sales department. And he

could make the decision to sell the jeans to me at a big discount. And now the new manager of that department is really difficult to deal with.

M: That's a big problem since demand is increasing, and if you can't supply anymore then your customers will go elsewhere.

C: Yes, I know. I've tried my best but now I'm **at my wit's end**[2]. Do you have any good ideas?

M: I think you can talk to the sales department again, show them how much potential business you have and how much business you have done. Make them understand that you are an important customer to them that they can't ignore.

C: Actually, I have talked to them seriously many times, but that new guy still pays no attention to me.

M: Then, I guess you have to look for other suppliers.

C: Yes, I am but it's always difficult when they know that you are selling online. They are more willing to sell it to the wholesaler.

M: Then it's their loss.

习惯用语 3

① sell like hot cakes: 热销　　② at sb.'s wit's end: 全然不知所措

M: 你那个在网上卖牛仔裤的生意最近怎么样?

C: 不像一开始那么好了。

M: 为什么? 去年还卖得很火呢。

C: 去年是。可是那个原本在我的供货厂家工作的朋友,现在不在那儿干了。厂家拒绝给我低价供货,而且还总是延期供货。

M: 哦,你的朋友是那个工厂的经理?

C: 不是,不过他负责销售部。而且他有权做主以大折扣卖给我牛仔裤。可现在那个新的部门经理特难对付。

M: 这可是个大麻烦。再说现在需求不断增长,你要是不能及时供货,顾客就全都流失了。

C: 是的,我知道。我已经尽全力了,现在真的不知道怎么办好了。你有什么好主意吗?
M: 我觉得你得再跟销售部谈谈,告诉他们你有多少潜在的商机,已经做成了多少买卖。让他们知道你是一个不容忽视的重要客户。
C: 其实,我已经跟他们很认真地谈过好几次了。可那个新来的家伙还是对我满不在乎。
M: 那我觉得你得找个新的供货商了。
C: 是的,我知道。可他们一听说我是在网上卖,就不愿意给我供货了,他们更愿意卖给批发商。
M: 那是他们的损失。

Questions 3

1. Did you ever sell anything online?
2. If yes, how did you do?

Chapter 4　Campus 大学校园

13　宿舍生活
Dorm Life

Background Information

　　Chinese dormitories are usually situated on campus although some graduate students might be sited off campus. There would be separate male and female dormitories with the entrance manned by middle-aged staff (called aunties and teachers) who can be strict and forbidding. Normally the doors are closed at 11 pm and opened at 6 am with no access in between. The electricity would also be cut off. The dorms would house anywhere between 4 and 8 students sleeping in bunk beds. Facilities vary but often there would be no air conditioning and no hot water for showers.

　　中国大学的宿舍基本上都安置在校园内，当然，也有一些研究生的宿舍是在校外的。男女生宿舍严格分开，入口处都有中年工作人员把守，他们相当严格。通常，宿舍大门会在晚上11点至次日凌晨6点间关闭，在此期间不允许进出，楼内电源也会切断。在楼内，每个房间都有上下铺床位，住4到8名学生。宿舍的设施各不相同，但通常都没有空调以及供淋浴的热水。

背景信息

Dialogue 1

Linda: I really hate my new dorm!

Jennifer: Why? What's the problem?

L: It's my dormmates. They make fun of my accent because I'm the only one from South China.

J: That's a shame. But there's nothing you can do about that. Why not just treat it as a joke and **laugh it off**①.

L: I would if that were all but because I come from a wealthy family they won't accept me as a close friend.

J: It shouldn't really make a difference whether you are rich or poor.

L: Perhaps they are jealous of my new clothes and laptop and the fact I have the latest iPod.

J: It could be that I guess. But I don't think it's a good idea to show off like that.

L: I believe that if you've got it; **flaunt it**②! That's my motto.

J: And I think that's the root cause of all your problems. They probably think you are **a spoiled brat**③ too!

L: Well, I don't care!

J: In that case, all I can suggest is that you try to find another dorm.

习惯用语 1

① laugh it off: 一笑置之，把…当作滑稽可笑的琐事而置之不理
② flaunt it: 炫耀
③ a spoiled brat: 娇宠的孩子，在家庭的荫护、家长的帮助中成长的孩子

L: 我特讨厌我的新宿舍！
J: 为什么？出什么事了？
L: 因为我的室友。她们老拿我的口音开玩笑，我们宿舍只有我一个是南方人。

J: 真糟糕。可也没什么办法。你就全当开玩笑吧,一笑了之。
L: 要仅仅是这样,我也就认了。可是她们从不把我当作好朋友,就因为我家庭条件比较好。
J: 你有没有钱并没有什么不同啊。
L: 也许是她们忌妒我的新衣服,我的笔记本电脑还有我的最新款 iPod 吧。
J: 我觉得有可能。但是像你那样炫耀也不是什么好事儿。
L: 我认为,拥有的,就要炫耀!这是我的座右铭。
J: 我觉得这就是你所有问题的根源。也许他们觉得你就是个纨绔子弟!
L: 我才不在乎呢!
J: 你要这么说,那我只能劝你找个新宿舍了。

Questions 1

1. Do you have a strong accent?
2. Do others make fun of it?
3. Do you flaunt your wealth?

Dialogue 2

Albert: Ted, I wish you wouldn't smoke in the dorm.
Ted: Why? It's not forbidden.
A: I know, but the rest of us don't smoke and we don't like the smell.
T: Tough. It's a free world and I mean to carry on doing what I want to do.
A: But there are six of us here and you should think of other people besides yourself.
T: So now you are saying I'm selfish! What about all the visitors you have disturbing the peace and quiet of the room?
A: I'm sorry. I didn't realize that they were disturbing you.
T: Well they do but you don't hear me complaining all the time

like you do!

A: Sorry, it's just that the other guys are really **fed up with**① all the smoke and they're also worried about the effects of **passive smoking**②.

T: Tell you what; if you **cut down on**③ your visitors then I'll cut down on my smoking. Is it a deal?

A: Sounds good. OK, you've got yourself a deal.

习惯用语 2

① feed up with: 极其厌倦（或不满）
② passive smoking: 被动吸烟，吸二手烟
③ cut down on: 减少

A: Ted, 你要是能不在宿舍吸烟就好了。
T: 为什么？宿舍里又不禁止吸烟。
A: 我知道，但是大家都不吸烟，而且我们也不喜欢烟味儿。
T: 真事儿吗！这世界是自由的，我想干什么就干什么。
A: 但是宿舍里一共六个人呢，你在考虑自己的同时，也要考虑一下其他人。
T: 你的意思是说我自私?! 那你平时带过来的那些访客呢，不也打扰了宿舍的宁静吗？
A: 我道歉。我没意识到那会打扰你。
T: 当然打扰我了，只不过你没有听到我像你一样，这么怨声载道！
A: 对不起，只是大家真的受够了烟味儿，而且也怕吸二手烟对身体造成危害。
T: 这么说吧，你要是少往宿舍带客人，我就少在宿舍吸烟，怎么样？
A: 好吧，我们就这么说定了。

Questions 2

1. Do you think people should smoke in dorms?
2. How do you keep the peace in a dorm when a problem occurs?

Dialogue 3

Alice: My dormmates are so vain and shallow!
Michael: Oh, why is that?
A: All they think about is clothes and shopping and boys.
M: I thought all girls were like that.
A: Not me! I'm more of a **tomboy**① than a **Barbie girl**②.
M: Don't you like shopping, then?
A: Sure, but I want to enjoy my freedom while I'm here, not be a **fashion slave**③ like some girls I know!
M: But we boys like to look at pretty girls who are fashionably dressed.
A: Well, go ahead then! But remember, there's more to a girl than just the outside, you know!
M: I know, but I like the packaging more! So am I shallow too?
A: I'm not going to tell you but I think you know the answer to that one!
M: What about boys, then?
A: There'll be plenty of time for that later. I don't want to be **tied down**④ just yet.
M: What happens if the right boy **comes along**⑤?
A: I'll **cross that bridge when I come to it**⑥.

习惯用语 3

① tomboy: 假小子，像男孩子一样的女孩
② Barbie girl: 巴比女孩，穿着时尚的漂亮女孩
③ fashion slave: 时尚的奴隶，疯狂追逐最新潮流的人
④ tie down: 限制，束缚
⑤ come along: 出现
⑥ cross that bridge when I come to it: 车到山前必有路，待到问题出现时再设法解决不迟

A: 我的那些室友特别虚荣浅薄!
M: 怎么这么说?
A: 她们整天只想着衣服、购物、男生什么的。
M: 我觉得所有的女生都这样啊。
A: 我可不是!我更像一个"假小子",而不像时尚女生。
M: 那你不喜欢购物?
A: 喜欢啊,可我想在商场里享受自由的购物,而不是像我所知道的那些女生那样,成为时尚的奴隶。
M: 但我们男孩子都喜欢看那些穿着时髦的漂亮女生。
A: 那就去看吧!但是你得记住,女孩子不能光看外表!
M: 我知道,但我更喜欢外表。我是不是也太浅薄了?
A: 这我可不好说,我觉得你知道答案!
M: 除了衣服和购物,那男生呢?
A: 以后有的是时间啊。我可不想现在就被牢牢拴住。
M: 要是你喜欢的男生出现了呢?
A: 车到山前必有路,到时候自然就有办法了。

Questions 3

1. What are your dormmates like when it comes to clothes, shopping and boys?
2. Are all girls really like that?
3. What do you think boys look for in a girl?

Chapter 4　Campus 大学校园

14　课程
Classes

Background Information

Chinese students usually have a lot of classes which start at 8 am and might finish in the evening. Classrooms normally have fixed desks and there would be a blackboard but there is a trend to update classrooms to include multi media. Often the start and end of a class begins with a bell. The usual size of a class would be 30 but it could be as low as 20 or as high as 40. Classes are really double periods of 45 or 50 minutes each with a break of 10 minutes in between. The academic year consisting of two semesters starts in September and finishes end of June or early July.

中国学生的课程很多，从早上8点开始，也许会一直上到晚上。教室内的桌椅都是固定的，还有一块大黑板。目前，许多教室都在进行多媒体化的升级改造。上下课都会有铃声提醒。通常，一个班内会有30名学生，少一点的有20名，多一点的会有40名。一次课由两部分历时45至50分钟的小节组成，中间会有10分钟的休息时间。一学年分为两个学期，九月开始，次年六月底或七月初结束。

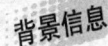

背景信息

Dialogue 1

Jo: You look tired. What have you been doing?

Emily: I've been **burning the midnight oil**①. Been writing my mid-term essay.

J: Oh no! I feel sorry for you. I thought you'd finished it already!

E: Yes, I did. But my teacher wasn't happy with it. She told me to do it all again!

J: No way! Your teacher is mean.

E: Well, I had to do it. Otherwise, she would have given me a low score.

J: I suppose if you look at it like that then your teacher is not mean at all. After all she gave you a second chance.

E: Yeah, and I have to admit that my essay is better now. I really need to do well so that I can get a scholarship.

J: Well, good luck then.

E: Thanks, and I'm going to **sleep like a log**② tonight!

习惯用语 1

① burn the midnight oil: 熬夜学习，开夜车
② sleep like a log: 熟睡，睡得死沉

J: 你看上去很疲惫，干嘛去了？
E: 我一宿没睡，写我的期中论文。
J: 天哪！我还以为你早就弄完了呢！
E: 我是弄完了。可我的老师不满意，让我全部重来一遍。
J: 不会吧！你们老师真够狠的！
E: 没办法啊，不然我只能得低分了。
J: 要是这么说的话，你们老师也还不错。毕竟她又给了你一次机会。
E: 没错，而且我必须承认，这次我的论文的确有进步了。为了得奖

学金，我必须把它做好一点。
J: 祝你好运！
E: 谢谢！我今晚得美美地睡上一觉！

> **Questions 1**
> 1. Do you have a lot of homework to do?
> 2. Do you sometimes have to rewrite it?

Dialogue 2

Michael: What do you think of our class?
Jed: I thought it would be great having so many girls but now I'm not so sure.
M: Why? It's every boy's dream to be surrounded by so many pretty girls.
J: Yeah, I thought so too at first but now I feel outnumbered and ignored.
M: You should be more active in class and then they will notice you.
J: I know but I just feel uncomfortable among so many girls.
M: Hey, look upon it as a social skill to be learned and an opportunity to make friends.
J: OK, I'll try but I feel so self-conscious among so many girls. You know, they always seem to dominate the class and **it's hard to get a word in edgeways**[①].
M: Hey, you're a man not a wimp! You should stand up and show them that you're not afraid of them and that you're better than they are.
J: Easier said than done! Anyway, **you've got no room to talk**[②]! You never say anything, either!
M: I'm just waiting for the right time, that's all.
J: Yeah, well me too!

> **习惯用语 2**
> ① it's hard to get a word in edgeways: 很难插嘴
> ② you've got no room to talk: 五十步笑百步，没有资格说别人

M: 你觉得咱们班怎么样？

J: 我一开始觉得有这么多女生会很不错，但现在不好说了。

M: 为什么？被这么多漂亮女生包围着，是每个男孩子都梦寐以求的事情啊。

J: 是的，我一开始也这么想，但我现在觉得女生太多了，自己有种被忽视的感觉。

M: 你应该在课堂里活跃一点儿，那样别人就会注意到你了。

J: 我知道，但是这么多女生让我觉得不自在。

M: 那你就把这当作是一项社会技能来学，当作是一个交朋友的好机会。

J: 好吧，我试试。有这么多女生在，我觉得很害羞。你知道，她们似乎总是在课上占据主导地位，你都很难插上话。

M: 天哪！你是个男人，又不是废物！你得站起来，向她们表明你并不惧怕她们，而且比她们还要优秀。

J: 说得容易！还好意思说我呢，你到时不是也说不出话来吗？

M: 我不过是在等待正确的时机罢了。

J: 那我也是！

> **Questions 2**
> 1. What do you think their major is?
> 2. Would you like to be in a class that's mainly your gender?
> 3. If your gender is a minority in class does that affect you in any way?

Dialogue 3

Jane: I really don't like Anna in our class.

Lydia: Why? She's a pretty and smart girl.

J: I suppose that's true but she's always **sucking up to**① the teachers and professors. Always trying to **be in their good books**②. She makes me want to vomit!

L: It's not a bad thing to be nice to teachers. Perhaps you should try it?

J: I agree and I do but not to the extent she does.

L: Sounds to me as if you are a bit jealous of Anna. If I weren't such a good friend of yours I'd say you were being **a bit of a bitch**③.

J: I'm not bitchy at all! Anyway, why should I be jealous of her? I'm prettier than she is and anyway my dress sense is better than hers.

L: Maybe Jane, but I think you should try to keep it all in perspective. You're not **love rivals**④!

J: True, but if we were I'd beat her any day!

L: Oh Jane! You'll never change will you!

J: Why should I? She's the one who ought to change, not me!

习惯用语 3

① suck up to: 奉承，巴结
② be in sb.'s good books: 讨某人欢心，得宠于某人
③ a bit of a bitch: 口出恶言的人
④ love rivals: 情敌

J: 我不喜欢我们班的那个 Anna。
L: 为什么？她可是个漂亮又聪明的姑娘。
J: 我知道，可她总是巴结老师，努力想讨他们欢心。简直令我恶心！
L: 和老师搞好关系不是什么坏事啊。也许，你也应该试试。
J: 我同意，而且我也在这么做，可不像她做得那么夸张。
L: 听起来，我觉得你好像有点嫉妒 Anna 啊。我要不是你的好朋友，我肯定会说你有点儿像个小泼妇。
J: 我才没有那么狠毒呢！再说了，我嫉妒她干什么？我比她漂亮，衣着品位也比她高。
L: 也许是那样，但我觉得你还是应该客观点儿。你们又不是情敌。

J: 嗯，如果我们是情敌，她一定不是我的个儿！
L: 天哪，Jane！你就不能改变一下吗？
J: 我为什么要改变？需要改变的是她，不是我！

Questions 3

1. Are some students more popular with the teachers?
2. Why do you think this is?
3. Is it a good thing or bad?
4. Do you have any classmates like Jane?

Chapter 4　Campus 大学校园

Campus　15 校园

Background Information

Campuses can range from the very small (e.g. Beijing University of Posts and Telecommunications) to the very large (e.g. Tsinghua). The main gate into the campus is usually the East Gate. On campus there would be the usual facilities such as teaching buildings, dormitories, library, sports ground, dining rooms, supermarket, etc. Most students would own a bike but often these are stolen. Dining rooms are cheap and crowded at meal times but the food is not of a high quality. Around 5.3 million students were admitted to universities in 2006 which was an increase of more than 10 percent from 2005.

大学的校园面积可能很小（比如北京邮电大学），也可能很大（比如清华大学）。通常，东门都是进入校园的主校门，校内一般会设有教学楼、宿舍楼、图书馆、运动场、食堂、超市等基本设施。学生们大多拥有一辆自行车，但通常这些自行车的下场都是被偷走。每到用餐时间，食堂就会变得非常拥挤，尽管饭菜的价格不算贵，但味道也着实不怎么样。2006年，中国大学的招生总数为530万人，与2005年相比，增幅超过了10%。

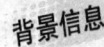
背景信息

Dialogue 1

Fred: Wow, this campus is really small!

John: Yeah, but at least it's easy to get to know it. I suppose you could call it cozy.

F: I suppose so but somehow I was expecting it to be a lot bigger. So I feel a bit disappointed.

J: Hey, **look on the bright side**①. The teaching buildings are close to the dormitory so we can stay in bed longer in the morning!

F: Right, so I don't need to buy a bike either.

J: I think that walking is better exercise than riding a bike and that way we can chat with each other on the way to class.

F: We can also **check out**② the pretty girls at the same time.

J: Cool, man! Great idea. Let's go for a walk now!

F: Right on!③ Let me just get my jacket.

J: I think I am really going to enjoy this small campus.

习惯用语 1

① look on the bright side: 看到好的、积极的一面
② check out: 仔细观察
③ Right on! 完全同意!

F: 天哪！这学校也太小了！

J: 没错，但很容易很快就熟悉校园。我觉得应该称之为"温馨"。

F: 我想也是吧，可我本想着它能大很多的。所以现在有点儿失望。

J: 嘿，看事情要看到积极的一面。这里的教学楼与宿舍楼离得很近，这样我们早上就可以多睡会儿了。

F: 嗯，而且我也不用买自行车了。

J: 我觉得走路比骑车更能锻炼，而且我们还可以边走边聊。

F: 我们还能在路上欣赏美女。

J: 酷！好主意！咱们现在就去转转！

F: 同意！我去拿件夹克。
J: 我想我会喜欢上这个小巧的校园的。

Questions 1

1. What would be the ideal size for a campus?
2. Do you find a bike useful on campus?
3. Do you like to go with your friends to class or go by yourself?

Dialogue 2

Sunny: I hate this canteen, I really do.
Juliet: Why?
S: It's always so crowded and the food's not very good, either.
J: Yeah, but at least it's cheap and convenient.
S: **Cheap and nasty**[①], you mean!
J: Hey, it's not too bad and it means we can enjoy a meal with our friends.
S: Well, that's one way of looking at it but sometimes it's difficult to get a table to ourselves.
J: Look upon it as a way of making friends by sitting next to a stranger and having a chat.
S: I know you're right but if I could afford it I would eat off campus.
J: Me too, but **beggars can't be choosers**[②].
S: What should I do then? I don't want to get food poisoning.
J: You could always cook your own or try a takeaway. I really love those **omelettes**[③] with meat and lettuce inside.
S: OK, I'll buy a lot of instant noodles and go on a tour of the takeaways.

> **习惯用语 2**
> ① cheap and nasty: 便宜没好货
> ② beggars can't be choosers: 没有太多选择的余地
> ③ omelettes: 煎蛋饼，煎蛋卷

S: 我讨厌这个食堂，真的!
J: 为什么?
S: 人特多，饭菜还不怎么样。
J: 但起码还算便宜方便啊。
S: 你的意思是，便宜没好货吧?
J: 还没那么糟。东西便宜，我们就可以和朋友常来吃啊!
S: 这只是一个方面，但有时候都很难找到张桌子。
J: 那你就把与陌生人坐同桌吃饭、聊天看作是一个交朋友的机会吧。
S: 我知道你说的是对的，但我要是有钱，我肯定不在学校吃。
J: 我也是，可是穷光蛋还有什么可选择的啊。
S: 我该怎么办? 我可不想食物中毒。
J: 那你就自己做，或者叫外卖。我特喜欢吃那种夹有肉和蔬菜的鸡蛋饼。
S: 好吧，我马上就买一大堆方便面去，正好可以去看看外卖。

> **Questions 2**
> 1. What are your canteens like?
> 2. Are there any good alternatives on or off campus?

Dialogue 3

Juliet: Do you want to check out the library?
Vivian: Sure. Let's go now.
J: It's so crowded, isn't it? I think we should have come earlier. We'll never get a seat.
V: There's some free seats over there. Come on.
J: Oh no. They're taken. They've left their books on the table.
V: I hate it when people do that.

J: So do I but **let's face it**①, we do the same thing.
V: I know, but I still don't like it. We'll have to find a classroom to study in.
J: I don't really like the classrooms. We could always go back to the dorm.
V: No way! There's always someone playing music and I just can't concentrate.
J: Come on, let's **grab a coffee**② and then we'll come back here later and hopefully there'll be some free seats.
V: OK, but it's your turn to pay!

习惯用语 3

① let's face it: 让我们面对现实   ② grab a coffee: 匆忙喝杯咖啡

J: 去图书馆看看有没有位子了, 怎么样?
V: 好啊, 现在就走。
J: 这儿太挤了。我觉得咱们应该早点儿来, 现在都没有座位了。
V: 那儿还有一些空位子, 快去!
J: 天哪, 已经有人占了。桌子上有别人的书。
V: 我讨厌用书占座的人。
J: 我也是, 不过也别说别人了, 我们不是也这么做嘛。
V: 我知道, 但我还是不喜欢。咱们找个教室去自习吧。
J: 我真是不喜欢教室。咱们回宿舍吧。
V: 不行! 宿舍老有人放音乐, 我都没法集中精力!
J: 来吧, 咱们回去喝点儿咖啡然后再回来, 但愿到时候能有空位。
V: 好吧, 不过这次该你付钱了!

Questions 3

1. What's your library like?
2. Do you often go there to study?
3. What do you do when you find a reserved seat?
4. Where are the best places to study on campus?

Chapter 4　Campus 大学校园

16　健康
Health

Background Information

Every university has a hospital or medical centre for its students. Currently, students have to pay anywhere from 5-20 percent of medical costs. The rest is covered by the university and the government. In Beijing, the government gives each university about 60 yuan per year per student for medical care. The average cost per student is about 120 yuan.

A good night's sleep is important for student's health. About 11% of students find that they don't have enough quality sleep while over 55% say they feel sleepy during the day.

According to the 2005 Ministry of Education report the average height of students was
- 172.5 cm males
- 160.5 cm females

Also 83 percent of students are short-sighted.

每所大学都为学生设置了医院或者医疗中心。目前，学生们只需要承担药费的5%-20%，其余部分由学校和政府来承担。在北京，政府每年给每位大学生60元的医疗补贴。而每位学生的人均年花费为120元。

夜间良好的睡眠对学生健康至关重要。大约11%的学生感觉自己的睡眠质量不好，有超过55%的学生在白天还感到困乏。

2005年，教育部的报告显示，学生的平均身高为：
- 男生 172.5 cm
- 女生 160.5 cm

同时，有83%的学生患有近视。

背景信息

Dialogue 1

Brian: Jack, it seems that you never get ill, unlike me. How do you stay healthy?

Jack: Well, I think good living habits are important to keep one healthy. Paying attention to personal hygiene will reduce the chance of getting a disease.

B: Yes, you are right. Can you give me some examples?

J: OK, for example, brushing your teeth well at least twice a day so you may not get any cavities in your teeth. Washing yourself regularly so your skin will feel more comfortable and clean.

B: So I need to go to the bathhouse a bit more often! And what diet should you choose to keep yourself healthy?

J: In my opinion, we should have a balanced diet to keep ourselves healthy. We should eat poultry and fish, vegetables, fruits and less meat and avoid food with a lot of sugar and animal fats.

B: Any other suggestions?

J: I think a regular sleeping and exercise schedule contribute to this. For me, I usually go to bed at 10 pm and get up at 6 am. Then I do some morning exercises like jogging around the campus. I have meals regularly. Besides, I will play basketball in the afternoon three times a week.

B: You really have a healthy life style!

J: A healthy life style has a good effect on ourselves. It can keep us in a good mood and feel alert and fresh.

B: Thanks for your useful suggestions. I think I should change my habits now and have a better life style.

J: My pleasure. I hope it helps.

B: Jack，你似乎从来都不生病啊，不像我。你是怎么保持健康体格的？

J: 我觉得良好的生活习惯对保持身体健康非常重要。注意个人卫生也会减少患病几率。

B: 嗯，你说得没错。举些例子好吗？

J: 好啊，比如，每天至少刷牙两次，可以帮你避免蛀牙。常洗澡，可以让你的皮肤感觉清爽舒服。

B: 那我得常去浴室！要保持健康，在饮食方面应该注意什么？

J: 在我看来，我们应当平衡膳食来保持健康。吃家禽、鱼、蔬菜、水果，少吃肉，还要避免吃那些含有很多糖和动物性脂肪的食物。

B: 还有什么别的建议吗？

J: 我觉得规律的睡眠和锻炼身体也对保持健康有所帮助。拿我自己来说，每天 10 点睡觉，6 点起床。然后做一些锻炼，比如在校内慢跑。我的饮食也很有规律。而且我下午还会去打篮球，每周三次。

B: 你的生活方式可真健康啊！

J: 健康的生活方式会对我们自身产生影响。这可以使我们心情愉悦，时刻感觉神清气爽。

B: 谢谢你的建议。我觉得我现在就应该改变一下生活习惯，拥有良好的生活方式。

J: 不用客气。希望这对你有帮助。

Questions 1

1. Would you say that you have a healthy life style?
2. What things should you do and not do?

Dialogue 2

Tony: Oh Frank, what's up? You look terrible!

Frank: I know. I don't know what's wrong. I feel lethargic most of the time and have **lost my appetite**①.

T: Doesn't sound good. Have you been to the hospital?

F: Oh come on! You know the doctors there only give you some pills and **charge you the earth**② for them! I'd only go there if I were dying!

T: Well something must be wrong with you. The semester's only just started so what did you do during Spring Festival?

F: Just the usual. Eating too much, late nights and not enough sleep.

T: Aha! I think I know what's wrong with you. You're suffering from post-holiday syndrome!

F: Rubbish! What's post-holiday syndrome anyway?

T: It's fairly common among people who've just come back from holiday. They did too much and didn't get enough rest.

F: Well, that certainly applies to me!

T: After a period of overeating you need to restrict your intake of meat or alcohol. Eat more vegetables and fruit, go for long walks. That will help you get your appetite back.

F: Anything else I should do?

T: Treat yourself to a **feel-good movie**③ and that will help relieve your fatigue.

F: Thanks Tony. You're better than a doctor any day!

习惯用语2

① lost sb.'s appetite: 没有胃口
② charge sb. the earth: 非常昂贵
③ feel-good movie: 一部令人愉悦的电影

T: 怎么了 Frank? 你看起来脸色可不太好!

F: 我能感觉到,我也不知道怎么了。我老是觉得昏昏欲睡,也没胃口。

T: 听起来可不太好。你去医院了吗?

F: 得了吧! 你也知道,那些医生只是给你几个小药片儿,就要收很多钱。除非我快死了，否则我才不去呢！

T: 嗯，你肯定是哪里出了问题。这学期才刚开始，你春节的时候干什么了？

F: 跟平时一样。吃得多，睡得晚，睡眠不足。

T: 哈！我知道你的问题出在哪儿了。你这是假期综合症！

F: 胡扯！什么是假期综合症？

T: 对于那些刚刚结束假期的人来说，这是很常见的。假期安排得太满了，没休息好。

F: 嗯，好像我就是这样！

T: 在一段时间大量进食之后，你需要限制肉和酒精的摄入。多吃蔬菜和水果，多散步。这可以帮你恢复好胃口。

F: 还有什么别的应该做的吗？

T: 看一部喜剧片，可以帮你减轻疲劳。

F: 谢谢，Tony。你可比大夫管用多了！

Questions 2

1. How did you feel your first week back after Spring Festival? Did you feel refreshed or worn-out?
2. What did you do to get back to normal?

Dialogue 3

Julia: Oh no Lara, I just don't believe it!

Lara: Calm down! Tell me what's the problem.

J: I've just weighed myself and I've gained 4 kilograms in just four weeks! How could that happen?

L: Hah! You've got "**Freshman 15**①". It's very common. Don't worry. You just need to eat less food and do more exercise.

J: But it's hard to say no to our dorm **snack binges**② at night. You know we like to treat ourselves after a hard day.

L: It's up to you but if you want to lose that extra weight then you need to ban snacks from now on!

J: But I'll become a **social leper**[3] if I don't join them!

L: Why not enlist their help? Just tell them you're on a diet.

J: I'll try. What else can I do to lose weight?

L: Make sure you have a good breakfast and try eating more vegetables and fruit.

J: But that will give me wind! I don't think my roommates will like that!

L: It's only until you get back to your former weight. And don't forget to take more exercise!

J: Yes boss! You can be my personal trainer!

L: In that case put your tracksuit on and we'll go for a run!

习惯用语 3

① Freshman 15: 指大一新生入学后通常会增长体重
② snack binges: 疯狂吃零食
③ social leper: 有社交困难的人

J: 天哪 Lara！我真的无法相信！

L: 冷静点儿！出什么事儿了？

J: 我刚才称体重，仅仅四周，我就长了 4 公斤！这怎么可能呢？

L: 哈！你这就叫"新生 15 磅！"这太普遍了，别着急。少吃多运动就行了。

J: 可要想拒绝我们宿舍的午夜"零食狂欢"实在是太难了。你知道，我们都想在忙碌了一天之后好好犒劳一下自己。

L: 那就看你自己了，你要是想减肥，从现在起就得拒绝零食！

J: 但要是那样的话，我会显得很不合群儿。

L: 你可以让她们来帮你啊。跟她们说你正在减肥。

J: 我试试。还有什么别的方法能帮我减肥吗？

L: 早餐一定要吃好，要多吃水果和蔬菜。

J: 但这样就会让人放屁，我的室友肯定不喜欢这个！

L: 等你恢复到原来的体重就行了。记住,还得多做运动!
J: 好的老大!你来当我的私人教练吧!
L: 那就穿上你的运动服跟我去跑步!

Questions 3

1. Have you put on weight during your first year?
2. How did you lose it?

Chapter 5   Family and Friends 家庭和朋友

17 独生子女家庭
One-child Family

Background Information

The Family Control Policy, commonly known as the "One Child Policy" was introduced by the Chinese government in 1979 to control a fast increasing population rate which had been doubling every twenty years since 1949. The One Child Policy advocated three main points: delayed marriages and therefore delayed child-bearing, fewer and healthier births, and most important of all, one child per couple. It stated that parents in urban areas were limited to having only one child while parents in rural areas were allowed two children provided the first is a girl.

从1949年到1979年，中国的人口数量翻了一番，为了控制急速增长的人口数量，中国政府于1979年开始实行了计划生育政策，即独生子女政策。独生子女政策主张以下三点，即晚婚晚育、少生优生，最重要的是一对夫妇只生一个孩子。据说，城市的夫妇只能生一个孩子，而在农村，要是第一个孩子是女孩的话，还可以再生一胎。

背景信息

Dialogue 1

Mum: What were your scores this semester?

Peter: 65 on average.

M: Why so low? What did you do in university every day?

P: But dad insisted that I study science, and you know I like western literature. If I had chosen English as my major, I would be the top student in the class.

M: If you **put your mind to it**① you could do anything! But you obviously haven't studied hard.

P: I have! It's just that I have no interest in science.

M: You know our family **expects so much of**② you. Who will look after us when we are old? We only want you to have a good future.

P: But English is the future!

M: Boys should study science, then you can find a job easily. If you study English, what can you do in the future?

P: I can do lots of things. Anyway, it's too late to talk about it. You always think you are right and never consider my feelings.

M: Dear, we love you and care about you more than anything else, and yet you never think about our feelings. Please try to study harder next semester.

P: Yes mum.

习惯用语 1

① put sb.'s mind to it: 用心做某事
② expects so much of: 对某人期望过高

M: 你这学期的成绩怎么样?
P: 平均 65 分。

M: 为什么这么低?你在大学里每天都干什么呢?
P: 但是爸爸坚持要我学理科,你知道我喜欢西方文学。要是我选英语作为我的专业,我就会是班上的优等生。
M: 如果你在学习上用心了你可以做好任何事!但你显然没努力学习。
P: 我尽力了!只是因为我对理科没兴趣。
M: 你知道咱家对你抱有多大的期望啊。等我们老了以后谁来照顾我们?我只是希望你有一个好前程。
P: 但是英语专业也有好前程!
M: 男孩应该学理科,你可以轻松地找到一份工作。如果学英语,你将来能做什么?
P: 我可以做很多事情。不管怎么样,讨论这个已经太迟了。你们总是认为你们是对的,从来不考虑我的感受。
M: 亲爱的,我们爱你、关心你胜过任何其他的事,你也从来没考虑过我们的感受。下学期试着学习再努力点儿。
P: 好,妈妈。

Questions 1

1. Do you think parents put too much pressure on you because you are the only child?
2. What's the best way to be yourself and yet care for your parents' feeling at the same time?

Dialogue 2

Emma: My sister is getting married this week.
Carol: You have a sister? You're lucky. I wish I had one!
E: I also have a younger brother. Didn't I tell you that before?
C: I'm afraid you didn't. I'm the only child in my family. I really envy those who have brothers or sisters. When I was a child I always felt lonely.
E: But it's not easy to get along with them. I still remember my

sister and I often fought over everything. And my parents love my brother more so he used to get the best of everything. So I envy you as an only child.

C: I think that more children make the family happier, even though they sometimes have arguments.

E: But I think the only child gets all his parents love. There's no competition.

C: Then the whole family **pins their hope on**① you. Sometimes it seems that you are always living **under surveillance**②.

E: I've never thought about that. But it means they think much of you, it's better than being ignored.

C: You don't know what kind of environment I'd been living in. I'm happy that I'm free now.

E: It seems that we both agree that **the grass is greener on the other side of the fence**③!

习惯用语 2

① pins their hope on: 对…寄予厚望
② under surveillance: 在监督下
③ the grass is greener on the other side of the fence: 这山望着那山高

E: 我姐姐这个星期结婚。
C: 你有一个姐姐？真幸运。我也想有个姐姐！
E: 我还有一个弟弟呢。我以前没告诉过你吗？
C: 恐怕没有。我是家里的独生女。我真的很羡慕那些有兄弟姐妹的人。小时候我一直觉得很孤单。
E: 但是和他们和睦相处并不容易。我到现在还记得我姐姐和我经常为一些事情争吵。我父母都喜欢我弟弟，他常能得到最好的东西。所以我羡慕你是独生女。
C: 我觉得孩子多的家庭更快乐，即使有时候会有争吵。
E: 但是我觉得独生子女可以得到父母全部的爱，没有竞争。
C: 那家里会将所有的希望都放在你身上。有时候似乎总是生活在监视之下。
E: 我从来没考虑过这个。但是这意味着他们非常关注你，总比被忽视的好。
C: 你知道我在什么样的环境中生活吗？我非常高兴我现在自由了。
E: 似乎我们都是看看对方的情况好！

Questions 2

1. What are the benefits of being an only child?
2. The disadvantages?

Dialogue 3

Betty: Hi Jenny! How are you? Why do you look so tired?

Jenny: Well Betty, our class has just been discussing a hot topic about whether having one child is good or not.

B: Oh, what was the result?

J: There are two main views. Some students say that one child for one family is much better. For one child can get more love and care from its parents. And they are healthy physically and mentally. Others say two children are better.

B: Yeah, but what's your opinion?

J: Well, I think two children are the best. An only child is lonely, and some are selfish because they always get what they want from their parents at home.

B: Hmm, I agree with you. That's why they are called "**little emperors**[①]". Are you an only child?

J: Yes, I am. I always felt lonely at home. So I wanted to have a brother or sister very much. What about you? Are you the only child?

B: No, in fact I have an older brother. When we were young, we often played together.

J: Great! I am a little jealous.
B: And because he is older than me he always takes care of me and looks after me.
J: Well, I will definitely have two children in the future.

习惯用语 3

① little emperor: 小皇帝（家里唯一的孩子，给他想要的的任何东西，导致过分溺爱）

B: 嗨，Jenny！你好吗？你怎么看上去这么疲惫？
J: 嗯，Betty，我们班刚才一直在讨论一个热门话题——要一个孩子好不好。
B: 哦，结果呢？
J: 有两个主要观点。一些学生说一个家庭要一个孩子好。一个孩子可以从父母那儿得到更多的爱和关怀。他们在身体上和精神上都很健康。其他的人为两个孩子更好。
B: 哦，那你的观点呢？
J: 嗯，我认为两个孩子是最好的。一个孩子太孤单了，而且在家里总是要什么父母就给什么，有些孩子就很自私。
B: 嗯，我同意。所以都叫他们"小皇帝"。你是独生女吗？
J: 我是。我在家总会觉得孤独。所以我非常想要一个兄弟姐妹。你呢？是独生女吗？
B: 不是，我有一个哥哥。我们小时候经常一起玩儿。
J: 太好了！我有点儿嫉妒你了。
B: 而且因为他比我大点儿，他总是关心照顾我。
J: 真好，我将来一定要两个孩子。

Questions 3

1. How many children will you have in the future? Why?
2. Would you ever want more than two children?

Chapter 5 Family and Friends 家庭和朋友

18 父母和孩子
Parents and Children

Background Information

Children are brought up to obey their parents in everything and parents will make the major decisions in life such as university, major, relationships and career. Mothers are seen as kind and loving whereas fathers are strict and a bit aloof. In China, a family is headed by the most senior person, either the grandparents or parents. Children come next, followed by brothers. Husband and wife relations come at the bottom. In the West, the order is husband and wife, children, parents and brothers and sisters. The husband and wife relationship is the foundation of a family.

孩子在成长过程中被教育要遵从父母的一切安排，父母会为孩子做出人生中的重大抉择，比如上大学、学什么专业、恋爱、职业。母亲总是和蔼可亲的形象，而父亲则显得有些严厉和难以亲近。在中国，一个家庭中最年长的人地位最高，比如祖父母或者父母。孩子其次，紧接着的是兄弟。夫妻关系最低。在西方，关系重要的顺序则是：夫妻、孩子、父母和兄弟姐妹。夫妻关系是家庭的基础。

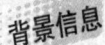
背景信息

Dialogue 1

Edwin: How's your first semester going?

Clint: Not so well really. I'm feeling terribly homesick. Right up to my senior school days I never spent more than a month away from my parents and I've been here for over two months now!

E: I suggest you do two things to minimize homesickness. First you should **keep in touch with** [1] your parents by phone, text message, e-mail or letters.

C: I ring them most nights, especially when I'm feeling depressed.

E: That's good. The second thing you should do is to **widen your social circle**[2].

C: How do I do that?

E: Chat with your roommates, study with your classmates and take up some team sports that involves you playing with others.

C: Why do you suggest that? They can never replace my parents.

E: They're not intended to. But the more independent life you develop then the less dependent you will be on your parents.

C: I see. I could also join some clubs and societies, couldn't I?

E: That's right. This is going to be your new home for four years and it won't be long before you've made some new friends and your social diary will be full.

C: And that means I won't be as homesick.

E: Yeah. Come on, let's find some of our classmates and **shoot a few hoops**[3]!

习惯用语 1

① keep in touch with: 与…保持联系
② widen sb.'s social circle: 拓展社交圈子
③ shoot a few hoops: 打篮球

E: 你这第一个学期过得怎么样?

C: 不怎么样。我非常想家。直到高中，我从没离开我父母超过一个月，可现在我已经离开两个月了!

E: 我建议你做两件事以缓解想家的情绪。首先你应该用电话、短信、电子邮件或者信件与父母保持联系。

C: 我大多数晚上都给他们打电话，特别是我觉得沮丧的时候。

E: 好。你应该做的第二件事是扩大你的社交圈。

C: 我怎么做呢?

E: 和室友聊天，跟同学一起学习，和别人一起参加一些团队体育运动。

C: 你为什么建议这些? 它们不可能替代我的父母。

E: 它们并不是为了替代。但是你越能够适应独立的生活，就越不会依赖你的父母。

C: 我知道了。我也可以参加一些俱乐部和社团，是吗?

E: 是的。这是你大学四年里的新家，你很快就可以交到一些新朋友，到时你的日程就会安排得满满的了。

C: 就是说我不会特别想家了。

E: 是的，来吧! 我们找几个同学一起打篮球吧!

Questions 1

1. When you first came to university did you feel homesick?
2. How did your homesickness wear away?

Dialogue 2

Calvin: What are you doing with your mobile?

Harvey: I'm deleting old messages.

C: Oh, why?

H: Tomorrow I'll go back to my hometown and stay with my parents for the May holidays. You know my parents will check my mobile when I'm not around. If they see Lisa's messages they will be angry.

C: Oh, I see. Your parents still can't accept Lisa as your girlfriend?

H: No, they can't and what makes me annoyed is that they also check my computer.

C: That's really not good. Why don't you talk to them about it?

H: I did, my father said, "I'm your father, I should know everything about you, what you are doing and what you are thinking."

C: Well, I think his motive is right, but his method is not good. We are adults and we have the right to our own privacy.

H: Yes, I agree. But what can I do? They never pay attention to anything I say, and they said they didn't have any privacy when they were young, so I should not have any either.

C: We are a different generation. I think maybe you should adjust your way of communicating with them too. After all, they are your parents and they only want the best for you.

H: It's not just the generation gap it's that they are completely **out of touch**① with the real world.

C: Then you'll have to **grin and bear it**②.

习惯用语 2

① out of touch: 跟不上新时代   ② grin and bear it: 逆来顺受

C: 你用手机干什么呢?
H: 我在删除旧信息呢。
C: 哦,为什么啊?
H: 明天我要回家和父母过五一了。你知道我父母在我不在的时候肯定会检查我的手机。要是他们看见了 Lisa 的信息该生气了。
C: 哦,我知道了。你父母还是不接受 Lisa 做你的女朋友啊?
H: 不接受,更让我烦恼的是他们还检查我的电脑。

C: 这样真不好。你为什么不跟他们谈谈?
H: 我说过,可我爸说:"我是你爸爸,我应该知道关于你的一切事情,你在做什么,你在想什么。"
C: 嗯,我想他的动机是对的,但是方法不太好。我们是成年人了,我们有隐私权。
H: 是,我同意。但我能做什么?他们从不注意我说的话,他们说他们年轻的时候没有隐私,所以我也不能有。
C: 我们不是一代人。我觉得你可以调整一下跟他们沟通的方式。毕竟,他们是你的父母,他们只想你好。
H: 不仅仅是代沟,他们根本就脱离了现在这个时代。
C: 那你只能逆来顺受了。

Questions 2

1. Do you often talk with your parents about your everyday life?
2. Do your parents ever check your mobile or computer?

Dialogue 3

Sarah: Where are you going?
Cassie: I'm going to a job fair. This is the last one held on campus before we graduate.
S: Wait a moment, I want to go with you.
C: Come on, your father is a departmental manager in China Unicom. He will no doubt arrange a good job for you. Why bother going to a job fair?
S: Well, I have decided to be independent from now on. I have thought it through carefully. To follow what my father arranged for me is easier and maybe more comfortable. But I won't have the chance to learn and will not really gain much experience.
C: Wow, seems you have grown up overnight!

S: Don't laugh at me, I'm serious. You've had a part-time job for the last two years and so you've been around a lot. But I still think like a student.

C: The reason I took a part-time job was because I wanted to make some **pocket money**①. Your parents give you enough money every month, that's why you don't have to take a part-time job. I'm sure you will never have to worry about money as long as your parents are with you.

S: But that's not the life that I want. I don't want to be dependent on my parents all my life. I want to make money by my own hand and my brain. I want to be like most other students in realizing my dream by myself. Maybe I will be more successful than my father one day.

C: Hey, I really admire you now. I thought you were a kid that could never live without your parents' help. If you want to be independent, you have to begin now.

S: Yes, I will get my CV photocopied.

C: OK, hurry up.

习惯用语 3

① pocket money: 零用钱

S: 你要去哪儿?

C: 去一个招聘会。这是我们毕业前的最后一场校园招聘了。

S: 等一下, 我想和你一起去。

C: 拜托, 你父亲是中国联通的部门经理。他肯定会给你安排一份好工作。为什么要去招聘会呢?

S: 嗯, 我决定从现在开始学会独立。我已经认真考虑过了。按照我父亲给我的安排, 工作会很容易也很轻松。但是我永远没有机会学习, 也不会得到更多的经验。

C: 哇, 看来你一夜之间长大了!

S: 不要笑话我，我是认真的。你前两年一直有一份兼职工作，所以你已经有一些经验了。但是我还是像个学生。

C: 我做兼职是因为我想挣些零花钱。你父母每月给你足够的钱，所以你不用做兼职。我相信只要你跟你父母在一起就永远不用担心钱的问题。

S: 但是那不是我想要的生活。我不想一辈子都靠我父母。我想用自己的双手和智慧挣钱。我想像大部分其他同学一样通过自己来实现自己的梦想。也许有一天我会比我父亲更成功。

C: 嘿，我现在开始钦佩你了。我以前一直觉得你就是个孩子，永远离不开父母的帮助来生活。如果你想独立，你现在就得开始了。

S: 是，我要去复印我的简历。

C: 好，快点儿。

Questions 3

1. Do your parents try to arrange your future?
2. Will you follow them or depend on yourself?

Chapter 5　Family and Friends 家庭和朋友

19　大家庭
Extended Family

Background Information

The Chinese word translated into English as "family" is *jia*, which generally means the basic family group, those who are related by blood, marriage, or adoption, living and managing their finances together. In a *jia*, the males are all blood relations. Sons live in their father's house with their wives, who have been brought in from outside the family. As soon as daughters come of age, they are married out, that is, they join another *jia*. The *jia* shares living space and finances. One male, the patriarch (the oldest competent male) has ultimate authority in all family matters. In the ideal *jia*, three, four, or five generations live under one roof. Sons obediently follow their father's direction in choosing a career and a mate, and every member of the *jia* works together for a single objective: sustaining and increasing the *jia*'s wealth and status. Such a large, multi-generational jia can grow to be very complex. In the *Story of the Stone*, virtually the entire extended family live together in one large compound and share a common destiny.

英文的 family 翻译成中文就是"家",这大体是指有血缘、婚姻或者收养关系的家庭基本成员,共同生活在一起,共同管理家里的财产。在一个家庭里,血亲关系以男性为主。儿子与娶进门的儿媳住在父亲的家里。一旦女儿成年了,她们就会出嫁,即进入另一个新的家庭。家庭成员共享生活空间和家庭财富。男的通常是一家之主,拥有处理家庭所有事物的决定权。在一个理想的大家庭里,可能会有三代、四代,甚至是五代同堂。儿子要遵从父亲的旨意来选择职业和伴侣。所有的家庭成员一起为了一个目标而努力:维护并增加家庭的财富和地位。这样的大家庭有时很复杂。《红楼梦》所讲述的就是一个生活在一起的大家庭共同承担命运的故事。

背景信息

Dialogue 1

Fred: You know Pete, we'll soon be going home for Spring Festival and I'm a bit worried about spending so much time with my parents.

Pete: Why's that?

F: Well, I was brought up by my grandparents and so I'm not close to my parents at all. So I feel a little strange around them.

P: Why don't you try to spend as much time with them as possible and just talk about every day topics?

F: But I really want to talk about my problems in life, study and relationships with friends.

P: You need to concentrate on **small talk**① first before you get onto **weightier matters**②.

F: Yeah, I know but it's just that I don't seem to have any confidence in talking about anything with them.

P: I know, why don't I pretend to be your dad and we can have a cozy chat!

F: I suppose it's worth a try.

P: Well, hello son how are you today?

F: Fine dad. What shall we do today?

P: Why don't we **have a go at**③ weeding the garden?

F: You'll have to tell me which are weeds and which are flowers then!

习惯用语 1

① small talk: 谈论日常琐事
② weightier matters: 谈论比较严肃的事情
③ have a go at: 开始做某事

F: 你知道吗 Pete，我们不久就要回家过春节了，和我父母待这么长时间，我有一点儿担心。

P: 为什么啊?
F: 嗯,我是我爷爷奶奶带大的,所以我跟父母不是很亲。我觉得跟他们在一起有点儿陌生。
P: 你为什么不试着跟他们多待些时间,谈论一些日常的话题?
F: 但是我只想谈生活、学习和人际关系上的事情。
P: 你先要集中说些日常琐事,然后再谈论一些严肃的问题。
F: 是的,我知道,但是我跟他们谈论任何事好像都没什么信心。
P: 我知道了,要不我来假装是你的父亲,我们来一次舒心惬意的聊天。
F: 我觉得这值得一试。
P: 哦,儿子你今天觉得怎么样?
F: 很好老爸。我们今天干什么呢?
P: 我们给花园除除草吧?
F: 那你得先告诉我哪些是杂草哪些是花草!

Questions 1

1. Were you brought up by your grandparents?
2. Do you find it difficult to talk with your parents?

Dialogue 2

Kevin: Who was that boy who brought you some clothes?
Wade: My brother.
K: Your brother? I thought you said you were the only child in your family.
W: Yes, actually he's my cousin. But we are very close and I regard him as my real brother. Both of us are studying in Beijing. He's older than me and looks after me all the time.
K: Oh I see. So you were close since you were very young?
W: Yes, we played together when we were young, and because our families were poor, I used to wear his clothes. Every time when

he grew taller, he gave his old clothes to me.

K: Did he bring some **second-hand clothes**[①] to you just now?

W: No, that's what my mother asked him to bring for me. And he also took care of my mother when he went back to our hometown while I didn't. My mother said he is her second son.

K: I really envy you having such a good cousin.

W: I do think I'm lucky. And I try my best to help him as much as I can.

K: Yes, you should.

W: His English is not good, so I sometimes go to his dorm to help him study English, and I introduced my foreign friends to him. He was very embarrassed at the beginning, but soon he got familiar with them. He was happy to be friends with them and his English improved a lot.

K: That's what we call brotherhood.

习惯用语 2

① second-hand clothes: 以前被别人穿过的衣服

K: 那个给你带衣服的男孩是谁啊？
W: 我哥哥。
K: 你哥哥？我记得你说你是家里的独生子啊。
W: 是，他是我堂哥。但是我们感情很好，他就像我亲哥一样。我们都在北京读书。他比我大，一直都很照顾我。
K: 哦，我知道了。你们从小感情就很好，是吧？
W: 是的，我们小时候一起玩儿，因为我们家很穷，我经常穿他的衣服。每次他长高了，他就把他的旧衣服给我。
K: 他刚才是给你带的旧衣服吗？
W: 不是，那是我妈让他给我带的衣服。他回老家而我没回去的时候他也照看我妈。我妈说他是她的第二个儿子。

K: 我真羡慕你有一个这么好的堂哥。
W: 我也觉得自己很幸运。我也在尽我所能地帮助他。
K: 是的，你应该这样。
W: 他英语不是很好，所以我有时去他宿舍帮他学习英语，而且还介绍我的外国朋友给他。他开始非常不好意思，但是不久就跟他们熟悉了。他很高兴跟他们成为朋友，英语也有了很大进步。
K: 这就是我们说的手足情谊。

Questions 2

1. Do you have any cousins?
2. How is your relationship with them?

Dialogue 3

Carrie: Oh, I really don't like Spring Festival, what about you?
Aileen: I love it. I can visit my two uncles and three aunties. They are very kind to me. And I will see my five cousins too. We'll have lots of fun.
C: That's why I don't like it. It's so boring to visit every relative's family **day after day**[①]. I sometimes feel I have nothing to talk about with them. Why do you have lots of fun with yours?
A: I don't know, maybe they are outgoing people and they like to make jokes all the time. The most interesting thing is we will make *jiaozi* together. Everyone will make their unique shaped *jiaozi*.
C: I see. I come from south China and we don't make *jiaozi* during Spring Festival. We eat in restaurants most of the time. My uncles and aunties like playing mah-jong very much. Every time they get together, they will play mah-jong from afternoon till night. I don't know how to play, so I just sit

beside them and watch. My cousins are very young. So we don't have much to talk about too.

A: Oh, that's really boring. You know my uncle is really funny and he has lots of ideas for games. Last time, he got us to do some IQ tests, and he would have small rewards for the most intelligent. So we were all eager to play with him.

C: That's great! You obviously get on with your relatives like **a house on fire**②. I think I will never have a good time with my relatives.

A: Well, it's up to you.

C: Up to me?

A: Yes, maybe next time when they are going to play mah-jong, you can suggest an interesting game, and if they like it you will have a good time too.

C: Emm, good idea.

习惯用语 3

① day after day: 日复一日　　② a house on fire: 融洽相处

C: 我真的不喜欢春节，你呢？

A: 我喜欢。我可以去看望我的两个叔叔和三个姑姑。他们都对我很好。我还可以看见我的五个表兄弟姐妹。我们在一起很有乐趣。

C: 这就是我不喜欢春节的原因了。天天都去拜访亲戚很令人厌烦。我有时候觉得跟他们没什么好说的。你怎么能跟他们那么开心呢？

A: 我不知道，可能他们都是外向的人，总喜欢开玩笑。最有意思的是我们一起包饺子。每个人都做他们特殊形状的饺子。

C: 我知道了。我是南方人，我们那里春节不包饺子。我们大多时候是在酒店吃饭。我的叔叔和姑姑非常喜欢打麻将。每次聚到一起他们都会从下午一直打到夜里。我不会玩儿，所以只能坐在旁边看着。我的表兄弟姐妹都很小。所以我们也没什么好说的。

A: 哦，那真的很烦人。我叔叔特有趣，他总是有很多游戏点子。上次,他给我们做一些智商测验,还给我们中最聪明的人一些小奖励。所以我们都喜欢跟他玩儿。

C: 真好!显然你跟你的亲戚相处得非常好。我想我永远都不可能跟我的亲戚愉快相处。

A: 嗯,这取决于你了。

C: 取决于我?

A: 是的,也许在下次他们准备打麻将的时候,你可以建议一个有意思的游戏,如果他们喜欢你也可以玩儿得很高兴了。

C: 嗯,好主意。

Questions 3

1. What do you often do with your relatives?
2. Do you like to spend time with your relatives?

Chapter 5　Family and Friends　家庭和朋友

20　朋友
Friends

Background Information

Chinese students make deep friendships throughout their educational life and will often have class re-unions. If a student asks a friend to do something for them, they will often do it immediately even if they are busy. Friendship means that the other person comes first.

中国学生在他们受教育阶段会建立深厚的友情，而且毕业之后还会经常举行同学聚会。要是一个学生请他的朋友帮忙做一些事情，那他即使很忙也会立刻帮忙。友谊的含义就是把他人放在第一位。

Dialogue 1

Kelly: Hi, long time no see. How have you been doing?

Cleo: I'm doing OK, how about you?

K: It's OK. I think we haven't seen each other since last summer.

C: Sure, it has been nearly one year. Why are you just OK? I thought you would be very happy to study in Peking University, which was your only dream in high school.

K: Yes, it was. But after I got in I felt a little bit lost and lonely.

C: Oh, what happened?

K: Well, in fact nothing is wrong but I just feel the university life is not as perfect as I expected. And the most important thing is I can't find a good friend like you, whom I can talk about everything with. My classmates seem a little distant.

C: It happened to me too. We used to talk very little in the dorm at the beginning. Every one seems to just care about their own business. I missed you and my parents very much and I even cried under my blanket sometimes.

K: Oh, why didn't you call me?

C: I thought you would be happy with your new environment then and I didn't want to **bring you down**①.

K: Hey, you didn't take me as a good friend.

C: I always do. That's why I came to Beijing to see you from Wuhan, isn't it?

K: But how did you get used to life in Wuhan?

C: I **broke the ice**② by sharing my laptop computer with my roommates. We need to use a computer to finish our English homework, so now they don't have to go to the computer lab every time. After that, we began socialising together and studying together. Our relationship is really good now.

K: Seems I should do something about that too.

C: Maybe, but don't forget me when you have new friends.

K: Of course not.

习惯用语 1

① bring sb. down: 使人感觉沮丧
② break the ice: 打破沉默, 使气氛活跃

K: 嗨, 好久不见。最近怎么样?
C: 挺好的, 你怎么样?
K: 还行吧。我记得我们从去年夏天就没再见过了。
C: 的确, 将近一年没见了。你怎么仅仅是还行啊? 我觉得你在北京大学学习应该非常开心啊, 那是你高中时唯一梦想的高校啊。
K: 是的, 曾经是。但是从我来了以后, 我觉得有点儿失落和孤独。
C: 哦, 怎么了?
K: 嗯, 实际上没什么不好的, 但是我觉得大学生活不像我期待的那么完美。最重要的是我找不到一个像你一样可以无所不谈的好朋友, 我的同学之间都有点儿疏远。
C: 我也是。我们开始在宿舍很少交谈。每个人似乎都只关心自己的事。我非常想你和我的父母, 我有时甚至躲在毯子下面哭。
K: 哦, 那你为什么不给我打电话?
C: 我想你可能在新环境中过得很开心, 不想让你觉得心情沮丧。
K: 嘿, 你没有把我当好朋友。
C: 我一直当你是好朋友。所以我从武汉来北京看你, 不是吗?
K: 但是你怎么习惯武汉的生活的呢?
C: 我开始打破这种僵局是通过跟我室友共用我的笔记本电脑。我们需要用电脑完成英语作业, 现在他们不用每次都去机房了。之后, 我们开始一起活动、学习。现在我们的关系特好。
K: 看来我也该想办法适应新环境了。
C: 是的, 但是有了新朋友不要忘了我。
K: 当然不会了。

Questions 1

1. Do you still have connections with your good friends in high school?
2. Have you made many good friends in university now?

Dialogue 2

Alan: Why didn't you answer me in the exam just now?
Colin: Hey, I really don't like to help you cheat.
A: We are good friends, aren't we?
C: Yes, we are. But that's nothing to do with being good friends or not.
A: Why? Good friends should help each other all the time. People say "A friend in need is a friend indeed" I needed your help just now.
C: Well, I don't agree with you. If I had helped you cheat just now, then I would not be a real friend. A friend in need is to help your friend get out of trouble but not put him into trouble. If I had helped you, you might be able to pass the exam but you still can't learn anything and you will never try to study hard.
A: Come on! It's just an exam. You know my father will beat me if I can't pass this exam.
C: Well, if your father beats you then **that should be a good lesson for you**①.
A: Now I really doubt if you really are my friend or not.
C: What I said and did is **for your own good**②.
A: Good for me? You want me to be beaten by my father?
C: No, you won't. There is another chance this semester. Let's go to the library this afternoon, I will help you to study. I am sure you will pass it next time.
A: Oh. That's boring.
C: Come on, don't be stupid.

习惯用语 2

① that should be a good lesson for you: 给某人一个教训
② for sb.'s own good: 为了某人好

A：刚才考试的时候你为什么不理我啊？

C：嘿，我真的不喜欢帮你作弊。

A：我们是好朋友，不是吗？

C：是的，我们是。但是这跟是不是好朋友没有关系。

A：为什么？好朋友应该一直互相帮助。人们常说"在危难之中出手相助的朋友才是真正的朋友。"我刚才需要你的帮助。

C：我不同意你的观点。如果我刚才帮你作弊，我就不是一个真正的朋友。真正需要的朋友是能够帮助朋友脱离困境，而不是使他陷入困境。如果我刚才帮你了，你可能会通过考试，但是你还是学不到任何东西，而且你永远都不会努力学习。

A：拜托！不过就是个考试罢了。你知道我如果过不了考试我爸会打我的。

C：嗯，如果你爸爸打你那就当是给你一个教训。

A：我现在真的怀疑你是不是我的朋友。

C：我说的和做的都是为你好。

A：为我好？你想让我挨我爸的打？

C：不是，你不会挨打的。这学期还有一次机会。我们下午去图书馆吧，我辅导你。我相信你下次能通过考试。

A：哦，好烦啊。

C：来吧，别傻了。

Questions 2

1. What's the definition of a good friend?
2. What do you usually do with your good friends?

Dialogue 3

Gary: Why did you ask Lisa out yesterday? You know that I've been fond of her for a long time.

Quinn: Yes, I know, but you never dared to ask her out, so I did!

G: Hey buddy, we are good friends, you can't do that.

Q: Yes, we are best friends but **all's fair in love and war**[①] you know.

G: Oh, well if you are in love with her then I'm at war with you!

Q: Don't be angry. Do you want to know what we talked about yesterday?

G: No! What you do is **of no concern**[②] to me any longer!

Q: Well, I'm going to tell you anyway. I told her that you have been fond of her for a long time.

G: Oh god, how can you do that? What did she say?

Q: She said she was quite fond of you too.

G: Really? Then what happened next?

Q: She asked me why you didn't tell her yourself.

G: What did you say?

Q: I said you were shy.

G: Ahh my friend.

Q: She laughed and gave me her number. Here it is.

G: Thanks good buddy. I will treat you to a good dinner tonight.

习惯用语 3

① all's fair in love and war: 爱情与战争一样，都是不择手段。
② of no concern: 不关心

G: 你昨天为什么跟 Lisa 约会？你知道我已经喜欢她很久了。
Q: 是，我知道，但是你从不敢跟他约会，所以我约了！
G: 嘿，老兄，我们是好朋友，你不能这么做。
Q: 是，我们是好朋友，但是你知道恋爱与战争一样，都是不择手段的。
G: 哦，好吧，如果你跟她恋爱了，那么我跟你就是情敌了！
Q: 别生气。你想知道我们昨天都谈了些什么吗？
G: 不想！你做什么我现在都不关心了！
Q: 嗯，不管怎么样我得告诉你。我告诉她你喜欢她很久了。
G: 哦，上帝，你怎么能这么做呢？她说什么？
Q: 她说她也很喜欢你。

G：真的？接下来呢？
Q：她问我你为什么不自己告诉她。
G：你怎么说啊？
Q：我说你很害羞。
G：啊……老兄。
Q：她笑了，并给了我她的电话号码。这儿呢。
G：谢了好哥们儿。今天晚上我请你吃顿好的。

Questions 3

1. If you and your friend liked the same girl or boy, what wouldwill you do?
2. Will you help your friend to date with a girl or boy?

Chapter 6 Travel 旅游

21 公共交通
Public Transport

Background Information

In cities the main forms of public transport are buses, taxis and the subway.

There are more than 20,000 buses in Beijing. Half of them use natural petroleum gas. There are 648 bus routes in Beijing that transport 10 million people each day. Beijing plans to open 50 new bus routes every year. In 2003, Beijing is expected to have 650 bus routes with annual passengers of 4.5 billion. Besides, there are 222 long-distance bus routes linking downtown area with suburban districts and surrounding regions.

At present, there are 67,000 taxis in Beijing. By the end of 2008, all the taxis will be equipped with a wireless telecommunication system and Global Positioning System (GPS).

在城市里，主要的公共交通方式是公交车、出租车还有地铁。在北京，有2万余辆公交车，半数都使用天然气作燃料。北京有648条公交线路，每天负责运送1000万名乘客，此外，还计划每年再增开50条新的线路。2003年，北京估计有650条公交线路，每年运送旅客4.5亿人。同时，还有222条长途线路连接着郊区和周边地区。目前，北京有6.7万辆出租车。到2008年底，所有的出租车都会配置无线通信系统和全球定位系统（GPS）。

背景信息

Dialogue 1

Martin: I'm finding it difficult to get a train ticket home for the Spring Festival. Last year I stood for 25 hours from Beijing to Chengdu so I need a seat this year. Any ideas?

Bob: The best thing to do is to try your own university first. They offer hard seats and their fee is only 5 yuan.

M: But my university's not on the Beijing Railway Bureau's list of 100 privileged colleges and universities. I can only apply as a member of a group and not as an individual. It's too much trouble so I'd rather try an agency or the railway station.

B: Well an agency may charge you between 20 to 30 yuan but sometimes they don't guarantee a ticket.

M: I'd rather try the station but there's always a long queue and it takes ages to get a ticket.

B: I heard some of the students getting their friends to go with them to queue. That way you **stand a better chance of**[①] getting a ticket!

M: I don't really want to ask my friends to queue all day.

B: If you don't want to queue then you can always try a **scalper**[②]!

M: If I can't get a ticket any other way then I'll try that.

B: You can try going online. I know there's a few sites that offer tickets.

M: That's worth a try too. Thanks Bob.

习惯用语 1

① stand a better chance of: 更有可能
② scalper: 黄牛党，票贩子

M: 我发现春节的时候要想买一张回家的火车票实在太难了。去年我从北京一直站到了成都，整整 25 个小时啊！今年我得买张坐票。

你有什么好主意吗?
B: 最好的办法还是先在你们学校试试。在学校里可以订到硬座票,只要5块钱的手续费。
M: 可是我们学校不在北京铁路局的100所重点院校名单之列。我只能等着团体购票,不能独自购买,太麻烦了!我宁愿去车票代理点或者车站买。
B: 代理点可能会收你20到30元的手续费,而且有时候他们还不保证能买到票。
M: 那我就去车站试试,可是那里得排大队,花好长时间才能买到票。
B: 我听说有些学生叫上自己的朋友一起去排队,那样买到票的几率就会大一些。
M: 我不太想让我的朋友陪我排一整天的队。
B: 你要是不想排队,也可以试试票贩子。
M: 要是我怎么都买不到票,我就会找票贩子的。
B: 你可以试试在网上买。我知道有些网站可以在线购票。
M: 这倒值得一试。谢谢,Bob。

> **Questions 1**
> 1. Do you find it difficult getting a train ticket home?
> 2. What's the best way of getting a ticket?

Dialogue 2

(In the bus station)

Linda: Hey, Kate **where are you heading**?①

Kate: I'm going to Wudaokou, and you?

L: Me too, I'm going to take some food to my boyfriend. We can take the same bus, if you like?

K: Sure, but why not let your boyfriend pay for a taxi, it's more convenient.

L: Well, the taxi driver overcharges sometimes. The first day I came to Beijing, it cost me 60 RMB from the west train station to Beijing Normal University.

K: Oh, that's really bad. Here comes the bus.

(On the bus)

L: Hey, granny, come and sit here.

K: I never give up my seat if there are young men around. They should give up their seat.

L: Come on, we give seats to old people out of respect. If others don't want to give up their seats it's because they have no manners.

K: Oh, last time, when I hurt my leg and got on a bus, everyone saw I was limping but no one gave me a seat. I was so disappointed.

L: I'm sure next time you will get a seat when you are pregnant.

K: Hey, what are you talking about?

习惯用语 2

① Where are you heading? 你去哪里?

(在车站)

L: 嘿,Kate,你去哪儿?

K: 我要去五道口,你呢?

L: 我也是,给我男朋友买点儿吃的。咱们可以坐同一辆车,怎么样?

K: 好啊,但是干嘛不让你男朋友掏钱打车去呢? 那多方便啊。

L: 出租司机有时候多要钱。我第一天来北京的时候,从北京西站打车到北师大,要了我60块!

K: 噢,那么糟! 车来了。

(在车上)

L: 老奶奶,您坐这里吧。

K: 我身边要是坐着年轻的男士,我就决不让座。他们应该先让。

L: 得了，我们给老人让座是出于一种尊敬。别人不想让座，是因为他们没有礼貌。
K: 噢，上次，我把腿伤了，上车以后每个人都看见我一瘸一拐的，可就是没人给我让座，我失望极了。
L: 我保证你怀孕的时候会有人给你让座。
K: 嘿！说什么呢你!?

Questions 2

1. Do you usually take a bus or a taxi when you go out?
2. Did you ever give up your seat to old people or pregnant women on the bus?

Dialogue 3

Cheryl: Which city has the best subway do you think?

Ivy: Well, I think subways are the same in every city. But Beijing is the oldest in China. Although it seems a little bit old fashioned, I still like Beijing's subway best.

C: Oh, why do you say old fashioned?

I: Because the tickets are sold manually while the subways in other cities are automated. What's more, some subway stations have protective screens, as in Shenzhen. This will be safer for the passengers who are waiting for the train.

C: Yes, that's really good. How about Shanghai's subway?

I: Well, Shanghai's subway covers most of the city with five lines. And the second line goes under the Huangpu River and connects with Pudong and Puxi.

C: Really? A subway under water! That's different. Perhaps they should call that part submarine rather than subway! I'd love to go on that.

I: Yes, me too! The first line was designed by a German but this one was Chinese designed. But Shanghai has the same design as Beijing. There are too many stairs in every station and transit stations. People have to walk a lot.

C: Come on, don't be such **a lazy bones**①!

I: But in Shenzhen, you hardly have to walk at all because they have lifts instead of stairs.

C: So why do you still like Beijing's subway best?

I: I think Beijing has more potential. It says that in 2020 Beijing will have the longest subway in the world; 561 kilometres long.

C: It will probably take a week to visit all the stations!

习惯用语 3

① a lazy bones: 懒骨头，懒惰的人

C: 你觉得哪个城市的地铁最好？

I: 我觉得每个城市的地铁都一样。但北京的是最老的。尽管有些跟不上时代，但我还是最喜欢北京的地铁。

C: 你为什么说跟不上时代了？

I: 因为其他城市都已经是自动化售票了，北京还是人工售票呢。而且有些城市的地铁有保护屏，比如深圳。这对等车人来说就安全多了。

C: 嗯，确实不错。上海的地铁怎么样？

I: 上海的地铁有五条线，覆盖了城市的大部分地区。二号线从黄浦江下面穿过，连接浦东和浦西。

C: 真的？在水下的地铁？这还真是与众不同。应该把那一段叫做水下隧道，而不是地铁。我想去坐一坐试试。

I: 我也想！一号线是由德国人设计的，但这条线是由中国人设计的。不过上海也有与北京同样的设计，就是每个站点和中转站都有好多楼梯，人们需要走很多路。

C: 得了，别那么懒！

I: 但在深圳就不这样，都不用走。有电梯，而不是楼梯。
C: 那你为什么还最喜欢北京的地铁？
I: 我觉得北京的地铁更有潜力。据说到 2020 年，北京将拥有世界上最长的地铁线路，561 公里。
C: 那要想参观所有的车站估计得一周的时间。

Questions 3

1. Do you often use the subway?
2. What do you think of the subway in your city?

Chapter 6 Travel 旅游

22 中国大陆
Mainland China

Background Information

China has three Golden Weeks in a year when travel is popular (May Day, National Day and Spring Festival). These three weeks account for 25 percent of the annual domestic travel market. 357 million Golden Week trips were made in 2006. The average amount spent by each traveler in 2006 was 447 yuan.

According to sohu.com during the May holidays people travel to the North 25%, Southwest 24%, East 20%, Northwest 13%, Northeast 10%, Central and South 8%.

在中国，一年三次的黄金周旅行非常受欢迎（五一、十一和春节）。这三周的旅行人数占据了全年国内旅游市场的25%。2006年，黄金周的旅游人数为3.57亿人次，人均消费447元。

搜狐网的调查显示，五一黄金周期间，游客的流向为：北部25%，西南24%，东部20%，西北13%，东北10%，中部和南部8%。

背景信息

Dialogue 1

Hugh: Which city in China is the best one to visit?

Quinn: That's difficult to answer because I think every city and area has its own special features. They say that Hangzhou, Dalian and Chengdu are the best cities to live in.

H: Well, I prefer old-style China to modern cities. I think that many Chinese cities are becoming the same. **All glass and concrete**① and no discernable Chinese-style architecture.

Q: Then Pingyao is the place for you! It's a traditional Chinese walled city. You'll love it there.

H: You mean all the walls are still intact? Can I walk on top of them?

Q: Sure. But the walls are about 6 kilometres long so you may prefer a pedi-cab.

H: That sounds like a good idea. What's the city like inside?

Q: There are about 3,000 courtyards although only 400 of them have been restored but it allows you to see what life would have been like in the past.

H: That's more **to my liking**②!

Q: You can also see some draft banks.

H: Draft banks! What are they?

Q: Chinese banks used to deal only in silver but in the early part of the 19th century they started to use paper drafts. This made it much easier and safer to transfer money around the country. One of the most famous banks is called Ri Sheng Chang and you can visit it and see where they conducted everyday financial transactions and also the storerooms where they held silver and other valuables.

H: I'll definitely go there when I've a few days to spare!

习惯用语 1

① all glass and concrete: 以玻璃和混凝土为主要材料的现代建筑物
② to sb.'s liking: 是某人喜欢的，适合某人的胃口

H: 中国的哪个城市最值得一去？

Q: 这很难说，我觉得每一个城市和地区都有自己的特别之处。人们都说杭州、大连和成都是最适合居住的城市。

H: 嗯，与现代城市相比，我更喜欢老式的中国。我觉得中国的很多城市都在趋于同样化。四处都是现代的高楼大厦，却没有清晰可辨的中国式建筑。

Q: 平遥古城肯定适合你！那是一座传统的中国砖墙小城，你肯定喜欢。

H: 你是说所有的城墙都完好无损？我可以在上面走吗？

Q: 当然了。不过城墙有 6 公里长呢，你最好还是叫辆三轮车。

H: 这个主意听起来不错。城里面是什么样的？

Q: 城里大约有 3000 个院子，尽管只有 400 个得到了修复，但你可以从中了解到过去的生活方式。

H: 那太好了！正合我胃口！

Q: 你还可以看一看票号。

H: 票号？什么东西？

Q: 过去中国的银行只经营银子，但在 19 世纪早期，便开始使用银票。这使货币在国内的流通变得更加简便与安全。其中，最著名的票号叫做"日升昌"，你可以去参观一下，看一看他们如何处理每日的金融交易，并且参观一下储藏银子和其他宝物的储藏室。

H: 能抽出时间我一定去！

Questions 1

1. Where have you been to in China? Which place do you like best?
2. Which place will you suggest a foreigner to visit in China?

Dialogue 2

Hazel: Of all the places in China I'd love to visit I'd have to say that Tibet would be my number one choice.

Nina: It's funny you should say that[①] because I tried to go there during the May holidays but all the train tickets were sold. I could have flown but with the new Qinghai-Tibet railway opening up that just has to be the only way to travel!

H: I agree! I know it takes two days but at least you can say you've travelled across the roof of the world!

N: And don't forget the marvelous views on the way. And then you arrive at Lhasa! I have a Tibetan friend and he says the best time to go is during one of their festivals.

H: When are they?

N: There's at least nine major ones and several minor ones. If you ask at the travel agency I'm sure they'll tell you.

H: It's really high up there. I hope I don't get altitude sickness!

N: Most people are OK so you don't have to worry about that. You're more likely to get a tummy bug. My friend was telling me all about yak burgers!

H: Yak burgers! What's a yak?

N: It's a kind of long haired ox. Tibetans put yak butter in their tea as well as eating yak.

H: Yak! Yuk! I **wouldn't touch it with a barge-pole**[②]!

N: Come on! Be adventurous! When in Rome do as the Romans do!

H: I'm not in Rome. I'm in Beijing. And when we get to Lhasa you can try it first!

习惯用语 2

① It's funny you should say that: 真奇怪，你竟然会这么说。
② wouldn't touch it with a barge-pole: 避免某事

H: 在我想去的所有中国旅游地中,西藏是我的首选。

N: 真有意思,你竟然这样说,我五一的时候想去,但火车票都卖光了,所以没有去成。我本可以坐飞机去,不过既然青藏铁路已经开通了,所以坐火车去应该是最好的选择。

H: 我同意!我知道坐火车要花两天时间,但至少你可以说自己穿越了世界屋脊!

N: 而且不要忘了一路上的壮观景色。然后就到拉萨了。我有一个藏族朋友,他说你最好赶在节日期间去那里。

H: 他们什么时候过节?

N: 西藏至少有九个大节日和一些小节日。你问旅行社,他们肯定会告诉你的。

H: 那里的海拔真的很高。但愿我不要有高原反应!

N: 大多数人都能适应,所以你也不用担心。你很可能会吃撑了胃。我的朋友跟我介绍了好多次牦牛肉汉堡。

H: 牦牛汉堡?牦牛是什么?

N: 是一种长毛的牛。藏民在茶里添加牦牛油,也吃牦牛肉。

H: 牦牛!哈哈!我才不碰那东西呢!

N: 别啊!有点儿冒险精神好不好!入乡随俗嘛!

H: 我没在乡下,我是在北京,所以不用随俗。咱们到了拉萨你可以先尝尝!

Questions 2

1. Have you ever travelled to Tibet?
2. Do you have any Tibetan friends?

Dialogue 3

Judy: I really need a break during the May holidays. Have you any suggestions for somewhere that won't **cost an arm and a leg**[①]?

Ellen: You know it's one of the Golden Weeks and so that's when everyone travels. You'll find that travel and accommodation are all more expensive then. I don't think you'll find any cheap deals.

J: I still want to go somewhere. If I stay here on campus another week I'll go **barking mad**②!

E: I know! We could go to the Goose and Duck ranch for the weekend.

J: A poultry ranch?

E: No, silly! It's a pub which owns a kind of holiday camp just outside Beijing. You can eat and drink as much as you like for only 500 yuan.

J: I don't just want to get fat and stagger around drunk all the time!

E: They have all these activities like horse riding, archery, all kinds of sports and even paintball!

J: Paintballing! I'd love to try that!

E: Yeah, me too! They even include transport from the pub and back so it's a real **hassle-free**③ holiday.

J: **Count me in**④! Will you ring the pub and make us a booking for this weekend?

E: Sure! I'll do that while you start packing.

习惯用语 3

① cost an arm and a leg: 非常昂贵
② barking mad: 疯狂
③ hassle-free: 没问题
④ count sb. in: 算某人一个，某人也去

J: 我五一假期得好好休息一下。你有什么好的建议吗？别太贵啊。

E: 你知道，黄金周的时候每个人都想出去儿。你会发现出行和住宿都特别贵。我可找不到便宜的地方。

J: 我还是想出去玩儿。再在学校里多待一周,我就该疯了。

E: 我知道。咱们周末可以去鹅和鸭农场。

J: 一个家禽农场?

E: 不是,笨蛋!是一个京郊的小客栈,那里举办假日野营。只要500块钱,随便吃,随便喝。

J: 我可不想发胖,也不想喝得醉醺醺的!

E: 那里还举办其他活动,比如骑马、射箭、各种运动,甚至还有彩弹游戏。

J: 彩弹!我很想试试!

E: 嗯,我也想!他们甚至还负责把我们送回来,这才是个无忧的假期啊!

J: 算我一个!你用不用给他们先打个电话,预订一下这个周末?

E: 当然了!你开始收拾行囊的时候我就打。

Questions 3

1. Have you ever been on this kind of holiday?
2. Do you think you would like it?

Chapter 6　Travel 旅游

23　香港、澳门和台湾
Hong Kong, Macao and Taiwan

Background Information

Hong Kong was handed back to the Chinese by the British on 1 July 1997. Macao was handed back to the Chinese by Portugal on 20 December 1999. China has a Department of Hong Kong, Macao and Taiwan whose main function is to implement, in the diplomatic field, the general and specific policies of the central authorities concerning Hong Kong, Macao and Taiwan questions; and to coordinate the handling of foreign affairs related to Hong Kong, Macao and Taiwan questions.

香港于1997年7月1日从英国回归中国。澳门于1999年12月20日从葡萄牙回归中国。中国设置了港澳台办公室，其主要职责就是在外交方面贯彻中央政府制定的，关于港澳台的大方针政策，同时协调处理与港澳台地区有关的外交问题。

背景信息

Dialogue 1

Scarlett: I really want to go somewhere different this Spring Festival. Where would you suggest?

Alyssa: I think Hainan is a good choice, but as more and more people go there during Spring Festival the hotels are fully booked and the beach is crowded. So maybe you can go to Hong Kong or Macao which are warm too.

S: But I heard that few people in Hong Kong speak Mandarin, and I can't speak or understand Cantonese.

A: Nowadays, more and more people study Mandarin in Hong Kong, and they can speak really good Chinese. What's more, nearly every one speaks English there, so you can also speak English with them.

S: You mean it's also a chance for me to practice English?

A: Why not?

S: That's good, and I am longing to visit Disneyland. But what about the cost?

A: It's not expensive nowadays. If you go with a tour group on a **package holiday**[①], I guess it will be about 1500 RMB per person for one week. But be careful to choose the right travel agency.

S: Yes, I will. Oh, will there be typhoons since its faces the sea?

A: Not in winter time. Typhoons usually attack Hong Kong in summer and autumn.

S: I see, so what's the weather like there now?

A: It's normally sunny and sometimes a little windy. So you need only to wear a T-shirt with jeans and bring a jacket **just in case**[②].

S: Thanks for the information. I will go there this Spring Festival.

> **习惯用语 1**
> ① package holiday：（由旅行社安排一切的）一揽子旅游，一切费用都包括在团费内的旅游
> ② just in case: 万一

S: 今年春节我特想去个不一样的地方。你有什么建议吗？
A: 我觉得海南是个不错的选择，可现在春节期间去那儿的人越来越多，酒店都订满了，沙滩上也特拥挤。所以，你可以去香港或者澳门，那里也很暖和。
S: 可我听说在香港很少有人说普通话啊，我不会说又听不懂广东话。
A: 现在，香港学习普通话的人越来越多，说得都特别好。而且，几乎每个人都说英语，所以你也可以用英语与他们交流。
S: 你的意思是这对我来说也是一个练习英语的好机会？
A: 对啊！
S: 好！而且我特想去迪斯尼乐园。那儿的消费水平怎么样？
A: 现在不太贵。要是你报团去的话，玩儿一周，我估计每人1500块钱就够了。不过你可得选对旅行社啊。
S: 嗯，我会的。那儿离海那么近，会不会有台风啊？
A: 冬天没有。台风通常会在夏天和秋天登陆香港。
S: 噢，知道了。现在那里天气怎么样？
A: 通常是阳光充足，有时候有点儿风。穿 T 恤和仔裤就行了，带个夹克衫，以防万一。
S: 谢谢你提供的信息。这个春节我就去那儿了。

> **Questions 1**
> 1. Have you spent Spring Festival in some places other than your hometown?
> 2. Do you have any ideas about spending Spring Festival in any places other than your hometown?

Travel 旅游

Dialogue 2

Jane: I've always wanted to visit Macao and now that it's back in Chinese hands I think this summer would be a good time to visit.

Sylvia: Do you know anything about it?

J: Nothing really. Do you?

S: My uncle lives there so sometimes I go and stay with him.

J: Really? So you can tell me all about it!

S: There are plenty of really old churches, but they're not the biggest attraction.

J: So what is?

S: There's an old fort and some excellent museums, but they're not the biggest attraction.

J: Come on, what is?

S: And there's some great Portuguese food and wine, but they're not the biggest attraction.

J: I'm going to scream if you don't tell me!

S: Not forgetting the Macao Grand Prix which uses the town's streets as a racetrack, but they're not the biggest attraction.

J: Come on, tell me!

S: Casinos. Now they are the biggest attraction.

J: You mean, as in *Casino Royale*? Does everyone wear dinner jackets and glamorous evening dresses?

S: Well, there is a **dress code**[①] but I don't think it's as smart as that!

J: Pity! I wanted to wear a really sexy dress, walk up to the handsomest hunk there, and say, "Bond, Jane Bond. 007. **Licensed to thrill.**[②]"

S: Oh Jane! You're impossible!

习惯用语 2

① dress code: 着装规则
② Licensed to thrill. 这里是一个双关语，因为在电影中，邦德常这么说。

J: 我一直特想去澳门，现在她回归祖国了，我觉得今年夏天是个不错的时机。
S: 你对那里了解吗？
J: 不怎么了解，你呢？
S: 我叔叔住在那儿，所以有时候我会过去陪他住一段时间。
J: 真的？这么说你可以告诉我关于澳门的很多东西了！
S: 那里有很多老式的教堂，但这并不是最吸引人的地方。
J: 那是什么？
S: 有一个老式的堡垒，还有一些很不错的博物馆。不过这也不是最吸引人的地方。
J: 别卖关子了，快说吧。
S: 那里有很多很地道的葡萄牙食品和葡萄酒，但这还不是最吸引人的地方。
J: 你再不说的话，我可就对你吼了啊！
S: 记得澳门国际汽车大奖赛吧？就是用城里的马路作赛道的。不过这也不是最吸引人的地方。
J: 求你了，快说吧！
S: 赌场。这才是最吸引人的地方。
J: 你是说就跟《皇家赌场》里似的？所有人都穿燕尾服和迷人的晚礼服？
S: 嗯，的确有一定的着装规矩，不过我觉得不会像电影里那样酷。
J: 遗憾！我还想穿着性感服装，走向全场最帅的壮男，然后说："邦德，简·邦德，007。"
S: 天哪，Jane！真受不了你！你也太能想象了！

Questions 2

1. Which of the above would attract you to Macao?
2. Do you think that gambling is a good thing?

Travel 旅游

Dialogue 3

Sherry: How was your exchange visit?

Liza: It was great, thanks! The weather was good and the classes were fun.

S: What were the students like?

L: Really friendly. I got invited to lots of parties.

S: So what's your impression of Taiwan's universities?

L: They're basically the same as ours but there's not as much competition to get in as there is here.

S: Oh, why's that?

L: Several reasons. There's the low birth rate, **brain drain**[①] and the fact they're building more universities.

S: Did you do any sightseeing while you were there?

L: I visited most of Taipei's **hot spots**[②] such as Taipei 101 and the night markets. In fact I got you this Hello Kitty doll from there. Everyone's mad about Hello Kitty in Taiwan.

S: Thanks Liza. So how long were you there for?

L: Only two months but I hope that with travel being made easier I can go back soon and visit all my new friends.

S: Yeah and I'd love to go with you too!

习惯用语 3

① brain drain: 智囊枯竭，人才外流（专业人士和受过良好教育的人士移居他国）

② hot spots: 热点景区，游客必看的景点

S: 你的交流访问怎么样？

L: 棒极了！那里的天气特别好，课程也很有趣。

S: 学生怎么样？

L: 非常友好。我被邀请参加了好几个聚会。

S: 那你对台湾大学的印象如何?
L: 基本上跟我们差不多,但不像我们有这么多竞争。
S: 噢,为什么?
L: 好多原因。低出生率,人才外流,而且学校的数量也多。
S: 你在那里的时候有没有出去玩儿玩儿?
L: 我参观了台北的很多著名景点,比如台北 101 大厦、夜市。你的这个 Hello Kitty 就是我从那里买的。在台湾,每个人都着迷于 Hello Kitty。
S: 谢谢 Liza。你在那里待了多久?
L: 就两个月,不过随着旅游手续的简化,我希望尽快回到那里,去看望我的新朋友们。
S: 嗯,我也想跟你去!

Questions 3

1. Would you like to visit Taiwan? Why?
2. Have you any Taiwanese friends?

Chapter 6　Travel 旅　游

24　出　国
Abroad

Background Information

In 2006 the number of Chinese tourists reached 34.52 million which was up 11.27% on the previous year. The most popular destinations for mainland travellers were Hong Kong, Macao, Japan, Thailand, South Korea, Russia, America, Singapore, Vietnam and Malaysia. According to a China National Tourism Administration report nearly 2 percent of Chinese travelled abroad in 2005. Most travel in low-price group tours of 15 to 40 people.

2006年，中国的旅客总数达到了3452万人，比2005年上涨了11.27%。对大陆旅客来说，最热门的旅游目的地为：香港、澳门、日本、泰国、韩国、俄罗斯、美国、新加坡、越南以及马来西亚。中国国家旅游局的一项报告显示，2005年，有近2%的中国人出境旅游。大多是跟随由15至40人组成的低价旅行团。

背景信息

Dialogue 1

Jerry: You look brown. Where have you been?

Ben: I went to Thailand during Spring Festival. I really wanted to get away from Beijing's cold weather to somewhere warm. So Thailand seemed an obvious choice.

J: Whereabouts did you go?

B: I went to Chiang Mai which is in the north. It's very popular with tourists as it's close to the hill country where you can go trekking.

J: So did you?

B: No. I only had a few days so I decided to go to the Golden Triangle.

J: Golden Triangle! What's that?

B: It's where three countries meet Thailand, Myanmar and Laos. It's famous for its drug trade involving opium.

J: I hope you didn't buy anything you shouldn't have?

B: Of course not. One evening I went to a kind of cabaret and there were several pretty girls singing and dancing. At the end they posed for pictures topless!

J: I hope you took some pics?

B: Sure did. Here, look.

J: I really fancy that one. She's gorgeous.

B: I should tell you one thing, though.

J: Oh no! She's a **ladyboy**[①], right!

B: Yeah! Do you still think she's gorgeous?

习惯用语 1

① ladyboy: 打扮得像女生一样的男孩

J: 你怎么晒黑了？去哪儿了？

B: 我春节的时候去泰国了。北京实在是太冷了，我想找个暖和的地方。显然，泰国是个不错的选择。

J: 你都去什么地方了？

B: 我去了北部的清迈。那里非常吸引游客，因为它靠近丘陵地带，你可以徒步旅行。

J: 你走了吗？

B: 没有，我没那么多时间，所以就决定去金三角了。

J: 金三角？什么地方啊？

B: 是泰国、缅甸、老挝三国交界的地方。因毒品（如鸦片）贸易而闻名。

J: 我希望你没有买任何不该买的东西。

B: 当然没有了。有天晚上，我去了一个小酒馆，那里有一些漂亮的女生唱歌跳舞，最后竟然袒胸露臂地摆姿势照相。

J: 你照了吗？

B: 当然了，你看。

J: 这个我喜欢。真光鲜亮丽。

B: 不过，我得告诉你一件事。

J: 哦，不！他是人妖，对吧？

B: 对！你还觉得他漂亮吗？

Questions 1

1. Have you ever been abroad?
2. Which country would you like to visit? Why?

Dialogue 2

Beth: How was your trip to Tokyo?

Hazel: Fantastic! I really enjoyed it.

B: What did you like most?

H: Harajuku. It's the fashion centre and caters mainly for Japanese teenagers. The clothes are really wild and **trendy**[①].

B: So did you buy any?

H: No! They are too extreme for me to be able to wear even in Beijing. Honestly the things they wear! And their make-up too!

B: They use too much, right?

H: Yeah, I think they go a bit **over the top**②. Can you imagine wearing black foundation cream?

B: I see what you mean. What were the Japanese like?

H: Very polite and orderly. They queue up for everything!

B: Not like here then!

H: No. And the streets are so clean.

B: Did you buy anything?

H: Only a few souvenirs and some comic books. Everything is so expensive there that all my money was spent on food and travel. I was broke when I got back to Beijing.

习惯用语 2

① trendy: 时髦的，时尚的
② over the top: 极端的，极度的

B: 你的东京之行怎么样？
H: 相当好！我很喜欢！
B: 你最喜欢什么？
H: 原宿。是一个时尚中心，专门迎合日本的青少年。那里的衣服特别夸张，特别时髦。
B: 你买了吗？
H: 没有！那衣服太夸张了，即使在北京穿也不合适。坦白说，她们的着装，还有造型都很夸张！
B: 她们太浓妆艳抹了，对吗？
H: 嗯，我觉得是有点儿过了。你能想象在脸上涂黑色的粉底吗？
B: 我明白你的意思了。日本人怎么样？
H: 非常有礼貌，有秩序。他们干什么都排队。

Travel 旅游

B: 不像这儿似的!
H: 嗯，而且马路上很干净。
B: 你买什么了?
H: 买了点儿纪念品和一些漫画书。那里的东西都特别贵，以至于我所有的钱都花在吃和行上了。我到北京的时候已经身无分文了。

Questions 2
1. What do you think about Japanese people?
2. Have you any Japanese friends?

Dialogue 3

Fawn: Come on tell me! What was your Paris trip like?
Zoe: Wonderful. I really had a fabulous time.
F: So is Paris really romantic like everyone says?
Z: **You bet!**[①] There's even a square called St. Michel where lovers kiss. They chew gum first and then stick it on the ground to prove their love.
F: Did you?
Z: I did! This French boy asked me if I wanted to and so I said yes!
F: Hah! He must have been good at **French kissing**[②] then!
Z: Actually he wasn't. His breath stank of tobacco even though he was chewing gum. It seems that most French people smoke and cigarettes there are very strong.
F: Did you go to the Eiffel Tower?
Z: Of course! I did all the touristy things such as the Louvre and the river Seine and the Notre Dame Cathedral.
F: Did you see the Mona Lisa?
Z: I did. But the room it was in was so packed and the painting

itself is disappointingly small so I never got a chance to look at it properly.

F: What did you like most about Paris?

Z: The cafe scene. Paris is full of cafes where you can sit outside drinking your coffee and eating croissants and watching people pass by. It's pure bliss. But one thing was missing.

F: I know! Your French lover!

习惯用语 3

① You bet! 当然！一定！
② French kissing: 法式热吻，舌吻

F：快跟我说说！你的巴黎之行如何？

Z：精彩之极！玩儿得非常开心。

F：巴黎真的像人们所说的那样浪漫吗？

Z：当然了！甚至有一个叫做圣米歇尔的广场，恋人们常在那里接吻。他们咬一块口香糖，然后把它粘在地上以证明他们的爱情。

F：你粘了吗？

Z：粘了！一个法国男孩问我是否愿意，我答应了。

F：哈！那他的法式热吻技术也一定是一流的了！

Z：其实不是。就算吃了口香糖，他的呼吸也带着烟草味。好像大多数法国人都吸烟，而且那里的烟草味道很重。

F：你去埃菲尔铁塔了吗？

Z：当然了！所有的必到之处我都去了，卢浮宫、塞纳河还有巴黎圣母院。

F：你看蒙娜丽莎了吗？

Z：看了。可是放画儿的那个房间太拥挤了，而且画儿本身也特别小，我都没机会好好看一下。

F：你最喜欢巴黎的什么？

Z：咖啡馆。巴黎到处都是咖啡馆，你可以坐在店外面喝咖啡，吃羊角面包，看路上的行人匆匆而过。这真是一种天赐之福。不过我

错过了一件事。
F：我知道！你的法国恋人！

Questions 3

1. Do you think that Paris is the most romantic place on earth? Why? Why not?
2. If you could go to Paris with a friend who would that friend be?

Chapter 7 Student Activities 学生活动

25 学生会
Student Union

Background Information

Almost in every university in China, there is an organisation called the Student Union. Generally speaking, the Student Union is divided into two parts: the Student Union of the whole university and the Student Union of each department. There are many departments in it, such as study and life department, gym department, entertainment department and so on. At the beginning of each semester, the Student Union will take in some new members. According to a 2005 Centre for China Youth and Children Studies survey 60 percent of students are or have been in a student organisation.

几乎在所有的中国大学里，都有一个叫做学生会的组织。一般而言，学生会由两部分组成，校学生会和各个院系的学生会。学生会下设很多部门，比如学习生活部、体育部、文艺部等等。每个学期初始，学生会都会招募新成员。2005年，中国青少年研究中心的调查显示，60%的学生都参加或曾经参加过学生组织。

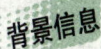

Dialogue 1

Cindy: Hi Ella, have you joined any of the Student Union departments? They are recruiting!

Ella: Yes, of course! And you? Are you in the university Student Union or in the Student Union of our school?

C: Well, I chose the university's. I think it is bigger so that there are more opportunities to meet more people.

E: Yes, that's right. But we are just freshmen, don't you think that the sophomores and juniors will **look down on**① us? They just tell us to do some little things! We can't really learn anything.

C: I think they do that **on purpose**② just to test you. If you do well on the small things then they give you more important things to do.

E: Oh, I'd never thought of that. I'd better **get my act together**③ in future.

C: So, you are in our department's Student Union?

E: Yeah, I think it's smaller, one knows others better and we can get along with each other more easily.

C: That's for sure. Then which department are you in?

E: The study and life department. You see, study is the most important thing in university and besides study, there is life. So I believe this department is a good choice for me. What about you?

C: I'm in the entertainment department. You know, I'm so fond of music and dancing and I like being **in the public eye**④. Given this, I think I can live a happy life there.

E: So both of us have found something suitable. Work hard and good luck to both of us!

C: Good luck!

习惯用语 1

① look down on: 轻视，瞧不起
② on purpose: 故意地，有意地
③ get sb.'s act together: 劲往一块使
④ in the public eye: 在众人关注之下，众目睽睽之下

C: 嗨 Ella，你有没有报名参加学生会的什么部门？他们正在招新成员呢！

E: 当然了，你呢？你报的是校学生会还是咱们学院的学生会？

C: 我报的是校学生会。我觉得它规模更大，有更多的机会去结识更多的人。

E: 是的，没错。可我们只是大一新生，你不觉得那些大二和大三的学生会轻视我们吗？他们只会安排咱们做些琐碎的事情！其实什么也学不到。

C: 我觉得他们那么做的目的只是在考验你。能把小事做好，他们才会给你更重要的任务。

E: 噢，我可从不那样认为。我还是等到将来再努力好了。

C: 所以，你报了咱们院的学生会？

E: 是的，我觉得这个比较小，大家更能互相了解，相处起来也比较容易。

C: 那是肯定的。你报的什么部？

E: 学习生活部。你知道，在学校里学习是最重要的，除了学习，那就是生活了。所以我觉得这个部门对我来说是个很好的选择。你呢？

C: 我报的是文艺部。我对音乐和舞蹈很感兴趣，我喜欢受人关注。考虑到这点，我觉得在这个部门里会很开心的。

E: 我们都找到了适合自己的。加油吧，但愿咱们都能顺利！

C: 祝好运！

Questions 1

1. Are you a member of the Student Union? Do you like it?
2. Which department do you think is the best? Why?

Dialogue 2

Stella: You don't look very well, what's the matter?

Amanda: I was so busy **handing out**① leaflets at noon that I didn't have time to have lunch, and I'm tired out now.

S: Why do you have to do such things?

A: I do it for the Student Union. We're going to hold a dancing party next week and we need to publicise it by handing out flyers.

S: Oh, I see. You're a member of the Student Union.

A: Yeah, to tell the truth, I'm **fed up with**② it and I want to quit.

S: Why? Isn't it a great honour to be in the Student Union?

A: But it's a waste of time. I really don't want to **mess about with**③ pointless exercises like this.

S: Come on, Amanda, there are many interesting things in the Student Union. It gives you chances to make friends and to do something useful for society.

A: Maybe you are right, but. . . .

S: Life in college is quite different from life in middle school. We should study as well as improve our abilities.

A: But I find it hard to balance both of them.

S: Maybe you can get help from some senior students.

A: Sounds like a good idea.

S: Why not go and get something to eat together?

A: OK, let's go!

习惯用语 2

① hand out: 分发
② fed up with: 极其厌倦某事
③ mess about with: 浪费时间做某事

S: 你看上去可不太好啊，怎么了？
A: 我中午一直在忙着发传单，都没时间吃午饭。现在都快累死了。
S: 你干嘛去干那个？
A: 学生会的任务啊。我们下周会举办一个舞会，所以要发传单宣传一下。
S: 噢，明白了。你是学生会的成员。
A: 对，跟你说实话吧，我都烦了，想退出。
S: 为什么？加入学生会不是很大的荣誉吗？
A: 但那是在浪费时间。我真的不想做那些毫无意义的事情，比如发传单。
S: 振作点儿，Amanda。学生会里也有很多有趣的事情。你有机会结识新朋友，做一些对社会有用的事情。
A: 也许你是对的，可是……
S: 大学的生活与中学大不相同。我们在学习的同时也应该提高自身的能力。
A: 可我现在很难找到一个平衡点。
S: 也许你可以从高年级的学生那里获得一些帮助。
A: 这个主意听起来不错。
S: 走吧，一起去吃点儿东西？
A: 好的，走！

Questions 2

1. Were you disappointed in any way by the Student Union? Why?
2. Do you find it easy to balance work and study?

Dialogue 3

Susan: Hi, Tom. **Long time no see.**[①] What are you busy with these days?
Tom: Hi, Susan. I'm so glad to see you. We're preparing for a chorus competition and it's taking up a lot of my time. I just feel exhausted.

S: Oh, I'm sorry to hear that. In fact, I wish I had joined the Student Union. In my opinion, working for the Student Union can help you discover **hidden talents**② you never knew existed.

T: Yes, at first, I thought so. But now, I feel that so much work has interrupted my study.

S: Oh, I've never thought of it like that.

T: Since I spent too much time on my work, I have no time to study. Sometimes I even miss class to finish my work.

S: That's a serious problem. Basically, study comes first for students.

T: Yes, so I want to leave the Student Union and focus on my study.

S: I don't think that's a good idea. It's all about time management. Do you want me to help reorganise your schedule?

T: Yes, please. I'd hate to leave as I know working for the Student Union will look good on my résumé.

S: A lot of students think that but we can't let your studies suffer. Let's go for a coffee and rework your timetable.

T: Thanks. You're **an angel**③!

S: Just remember me when you're the CEO of a big company!

习惯用语 3

① Long time no see. 好久不见。
② hidden talents: 潜能
③ an angel: 帮助你的人

S: 嗨 Tom。好久不见。你最近在忙什么?

T: 嗨 Susan。很高兴见到你。我们正在准备一个合唱比赛,花了我很多时间。我都筋疲力尽了。

S: 噢,真可怜。其实我真希望自己加入了学生会。我觉得为学生会工作可以帮助你发现自己拥有的潜能。

T: 是,起初我也这么想。但现在,我觉得这么多的工作已经干扰了我的学习。

S: 噢!我可从没想到过这个。

T: 我花了太多时间在工作上,都没时间学习了。有时候我甚至为了完成工作而旷课。

S: 这可是个严重的问题。毕竟对学生来说,学习是第一位的。

T: 是的。所以我想退出学生会,专心学习。

S: 我觉得这个主意不怎么样。这完全就是一个时间管理的问题。需不需要我来帮你重新规划一下时间表?

T: 需要。我并不想离开,因为我知道学生会的工作经历会为我的简历增色不少。

S: 好多学生都这样认为。但是你可不能牺牲学业。咱们一起去喝杯咖啡,重新规划一下你的时间表。

T: 谢谢!你真帮了我一个大忙。

S: 等你成了大公司的 CEO 可别忘了我。

Questions 3

1. Do student union activities take up a lot of your time?
2. Do you think some students join because of future career motives?

Chapter 7 Student Activities 学生活动

Sports 26 运动

Background Information

All kinds of sports are popular on campus. Perhaps the most popular are basketball, badminton and table tennis. Many team games are organised by classes so the quality of team play can vary considerably. As English major students are predominantly female this often means that boys cannot field a full basketball or football team.

在大学校园里，各类运动都很流行。不过，最热门的可能当属篮球、羽毛球和乒乓球。许多需要团体参加的项目都是由班级组队，所以水平也就参差不齐。英语专业的学生大多都是女生，这就意味着，班里的男生们都不够组成一支篮球队或足球队。

Dialogue 1

Belinda: Let's have a break, I'm so tired.
Dawn: Weak girl, we've only just started!
B: Funny, girl! Who taught you to play badminton? You seem like an expert.
D: No, I'm not, but my cousin is. He taught me.
B: So can you tell me some secrets?
D: There is no secret, just practice.
B: I'm sure there must be. I think I have been playing as long as you, but still I can't **catch up with**[①] you.
D: Well, I think your problem is you don't use your strength in the right place. That's why you got tired without making any progress.
B: Then where should I use my strength?
D: You should use your wrist instead of your arm to move the racquet. Otherwise the shuttlecock won't fly fast and you get tired easily.
B: I see, I thought the arm has more strength than the wrist.
D: It does but not in playing badminton.
B: OK, I'll remember that. Then what else?
D: Don't stand straight all the time, try to bend down a little so that you can move easily when the shuttlecock comes to you.
B: Oh, I'm always preparing to jump up.
D: That's why I usually give you a low shot and you miss it. It's knowing **the finer points**[②] of the game that gives you an advantage over your opponent.
B: I understand now. Hey, let's start to play now. I want to put those ideas into practice!

> **习惯用语 1**
>
> ① catch up with: 赶上　　　② the finer points: 微妙难解之处

B: 歇会儿吧,我太累了。

D: 小姑娘,我们才刚刚开始啊!

B: 大姐!谁教的你羽毛球啊?你怎么跟专家似的!

D: 我可不是,我表哥是。他教的我。

B: 告诉我一些秘诀好吗?

D: 没有秘诀,就是要练习。

B: 肯定有秘诀!咱俩开始打球的时间差不多,但现在我还是追不上你。

D: 嗯,我觉得你的问题在于用力的部位不对。这就是毫无进展还很累的原因。

B: 那我应该哪里用力?

D: 你应该用手腕来移动球拍,而不是胳膊。否则,不但球速不快,你还会很累。

B: 明白了。我觉得胳膊比手腕更有力。

D: 这是事实,可是打羽毛球的时候可不是这样。

B: 好的,记住了,别的呢?

D: 别总是站得那么直,稍微弯一点身子,那样当球过来的时候你更容易移动身体。

B: 噢,我老是随时准备起跳。

D: 所以我才老给你打低球,而你却接不到。所以,你必须了解这项运动的微妙之处,这样你才能赢对手。

B: 我明白了。咱们开始吧。我得把刚才你说的付诸实践。

> **Questions 1**
>
> 1. Do you know the finer points of badminton?
> 2. How could you improve your mastery of a sport?

Dialogue 2

Justin: I'm really interested in football but some of the **jargon**① used really confuses me. Can you explain it to me?

Nick: OK. Let's start with the players. They're usually divided into three groups. First of all, there's the defence which consists of a goalkeeper, a right back, a left back and then two centre backs.

J: Then you have midfield, right?

N: Yeah. Two central midfield players and a right and a left winger.

J: That just leaves two players if my maths is correct.

N: It is. Two strikers, but one is called the centre forward.

J: OK. That's the players dealt with. What about terms associated with the game?

N: Well, players score a goal. If a player scores two goals it's called a brace. If a player scores three goals in a match then that's called a hat-trick.

J: Why's it called that?

N: Apparently in the old days before players were paid, if they scored three goals then a hat was passed round the crowd who contributed some money and then it was given to the player.

J: Any other historical facts?

N: The game is divided into two halves. Before the official rules **came into being**② most teams had their own rules. So they used to play one half according to one team's rules and then the second half according to the other's.

J: That sounds fair, anyway.

习惯用语 2

① jargon: 行话，术语   ② came into being: 形成

J: 我对足球特感兴趣,可是我老搞不清那些技术用语,你能给我解释一下吗?

N: 好啊,咱们从球员开始说起。他们通常分为三组,首先是防守组,由守门员,一名左后卫,一名右后卫,还有两名中后卫组成。

J: 然后就是中场部分,对吗?

N: 是的。两个中前卫,左右边锋各一个。

J: 要是我没算错的话,就只剩下两名队员了。

N: 对。两名进攻队员,其中一个叫做中锋。

J: 哦,这就是队员的排列。比赛规则是什么呢?

N: 嗯,队员靠进球来得分。如果在一场比赛中,一名队员进了两个球,就叫做"梅开二度",要是进了三个球,则被叫做"帽子戏法"。

J: 为什么这么叫啊?

N: 在早些时候,球员并没有酬劳,要是他能够在比赛中射进三个球,人们就会在观众席中传递一个帽子,在里面放钱,送给进球的球员。

J: 还有什么其他的历史典故吗?

N: 一场比赛分为两个半场。在官方规则制定之前,大部分球队都有自己的规则。所以,通常上半场比赛遵守一个球队的规则,下半场遵守另一个球队的规则。

J: 这听起来倒挺公平的。

Questions 2

1. Are you familiar with the terms used in football?
2. Which team do you support?

Dialogue 3

Belinda: Would you like to play basketball with me this afternoon?

Emma: No, I don't. Basketball is a sport for boys. I don't want my body to be like a man's unless playing basketball somehow makes me taller!

B: If that really happened then I think all girls would play it.

E: Why do you like to play basketball?

B: You know when you play basketball, you will run a lot. In this way you can lose a lot of weight.

E: Well, that sounds good.

B: And because you have to think all the time when you play, it can improve your brain as well.

E: Do you think my brain doesn't work well?

B: I didn't say that, but it's good to make it work better, right? It's also good for eye-hand coordination.

E: Eye-hand coordination! What's that?

B: Well, you have to keep an eye on the ball using your hand as well so both eyes and hands have to work together.

E: OK. You've convinced me. Let's go and **shoot a few hoops**[①]!

习惯用语 3

① shoot a few hoops: 打篮球

B: 今天下午和我一起打篮球怎么样?

E: 不,我不打。篮球是男孩子的运动。我可不想让我的身体跟男人一样,除非打篮球能让我长高一点儿。

B: 要真能长高的话,我估计所有的女孩子就都去打篮球了。

E: 你为什么喜欢打篮球啊?

B: 打篮球的时候需要不停的跑动,这样可以减肥啊。

E: 听起来不错。

B: 而且你在打球的时候需要不停地动脑筋,所以这对你的大脑也有好处。

E: 你觉得我的脑子有问题吗?

B: 我不是那个意思。让头脑更灵活总是好的吧？对手眼配合也有好处。
E: 手眼配合？什么意思？
B: 你的眼睛得时刻盯着球，还要用手。所以手和眼就要在一起配合使用。
E: 唉，你真是把我给说动了。咱们打篮球去吧！

Questions 3

1. If you are a girl, will you play basketball?
2. Which sports are good for eye-hand coordination?

Chapter 7 Student Activities 学生活动

27 丢东西
Lost and Found

Background Information

Many things go missing on campus. Perhaps the most common things are bicycles. A recent survey by a Renmin University student found that on average each student lost 2.3 bikes. According to a 2003 survey by Beijing University of Chemical Technology the percentages of offences committed by university students in Beijing was

- theft 67%
- physical assault 19%
- fraud 9%
- sex offence 5%

在大学里，很多东西都可能丢失。最常见的，莫过于丢失自行车。最近，中国人民大学的学生调查发现，平均每名学生会丢失2.3辆自行车。根据2003年北京化工大学的调查，北京大学生犯罪比例为：

- 盗窃 67%
- 人身攻击 19%
- 欺诈 9%
- 性侵犯 5%

背景信息

173

Dialogue 1

Forrest: Hey look, this is the bike I lost last week.

Don: It looks similar to yours, but I remember your saddle was black and this one is white.

F: You're right, I guess someone stole it and changed the saddle.

D: And other than that, it's exactly like your lost bike.

F: Yes, I'm sure it is.

D: What should we do now? The lock has been changed so we can't take it away now.

F: How about calling a policeman?

D: But we have no proof to show this bike belongs to you. How can we make a policeman believe us?

F: Or, maybe we can wait here and see who will come **to pick up**[①] this bike.

D: OK.

(After one hour a girl comes to take the bike)

Forrest: Hey, this bike looks nice, where did you buy it?

Girl: Thank you. I bought it from a man who sells second-hand bikes.

F: Oh, I see. Do you still have his address and telephone number?

G: I only have his telephone number. I don't know his address.

F: It's OK, but I think that man is a thief.

G: Thief?

F: Yes, you know this is my bike in fact. I lost it last week. I think that guy stole my bike and sold it to you.

G: Oh, I know nothing about that.

F: Don't worry. It's not your fault. But can you **do us a favour**[②] by going to the security office and tell them what that

guy looks like, so that they may help us to find the thief?
G: OK. No problem.

习惯用语 1

① to pick up: 取东西　　② do sb. a favour: 帮助某人

F: 嘿！你看！这就是我上个礼拜丢的那辆车。
D: 看着跟你的差不多，不过我记得你的车座子是黑的，但这个是白的。
F: 没错，我估计有人把车偷走以后换了个车座子。
D: 除了这个，跟你丢的那辆车完全一样。
F: 嗯，我确信就是这辆！
D: 我们应该怎么做？车锁换了，我们现在没法把车推走。
F: 报警怎么样？
D: 可我们没有证据来证明这辆车属于你啊。怎么才能让警察相信我们呢？
F: 嗯，那我们就在这里等，看谁来取走这辆车。
D: 好的。
（一小时之后，一个女孩来取这辆车）
F: 嘿，这辆车挺好看的，哪儿买的？
G: 谢谢！我从一个卖二手车的男人那里买的。
F: 噢，你还有那个男人的地址或电话吗？
G: 我只有他的电话号码，不知道他的地址。
F: 好的，我觉得那个人是个小偷。
G: 小偷？
F: 对，事实上，这辆车是我的。上周被偷了。我觉得就是那个人偷了我的车然后卖给你。
G: 噢！我不清楚。
F: 别着急。这不是你的错。不过，你能不能帮我个忙，到校保卫处去描述一下那个人的相貌特征，以便他们找到那个小偷？
G: 好的，没问题。

Questions 1

1. Did you ever trace a stolen bike?
2. If not, where do you think your bike is now?

Dialogue 2

Helen: I can't find my bike anywhere!

Tracey: Are you sure you looked everywhere?

H: Yeah. I've **looked in every corner**① of the campus but it's nowhere to be seen.

T: So what will you do?

H: I guess I'll just have to buy a cheap second-hand bike.

T: You realize that will have been stolen too! If you buy second-hand then you're just encouraging the thieves.

H: But what can I do! I need a bike to get around.

T: Well, so long as you get a good lock you should be OK.

H: That reminds me of a story. A student who didn't want his bike to be stolen got three new locks for his bike.

T: But it still got stolen, right?

H: No. The bike was left but the locks were taken.

T: Why? What was the reason?

H: The thief left a note saying, "Your bike is not worth stealing but the locks are!"

习惯用语 2

① look in every corner: 四处寻找

H: 我的自行车找不到了!
T: 你好好找了吗?
H: 是的! 我找遍了校园所有的地方都找不到。

T: 那现在应该做什么?
H: 我想我应该买辆便宜的二手车。
T: 你知道,那可能还会被偷。你买二手车,就等于在鼓励那些小偷。
H: 那我该怎么办? 我出行需要自行车啊。
T: 哦,要是你有一把好车锁的话车就不会丢了。
H: 这倒让我想起一个故事来。一个学生为了自行车不被偷,锁了三把新锁。
T: 但还是被偷了,对吗?
H: 没有。车留下了,但是锁被偷走了。
T: 为什么?
H: 小偷留下了一张纸条,说:"你的车不值一偷,不过这些锁还不错。"

Questions 2

1. Do you ever buy second-hand bikes?
2. What do you think can be done to stop bike thieves on campus?

Dialogue 3

Elliot: Hi Gavin. What's happened? Why are you looking so worried?

Gavin: Have you seen my MP4?

E: Your MP4? No. Didn't you use it yesterday?

G: Well, I did. But it's gone now. I've turned our dorm **upside down**[①] trying to find it, but it....

E: So, you mean someone must have taken it. Right?

G: Maybe, but it was me who was the last one who left our room this morning. And, I remember clearly that I locked the door. And what is more, there are two doorkeepers so how can the thief get inside our building?

E: I don't know. But, why not ask them to check the **cctv**[②]?

Maybe you can see something useful.

G: It's my only chance.

(At reception)

Gavin: Hello, sir. I am a student living in room 236, and my MP4 has disappeared and I think someone has taken it. Would you please check the cctv? I left this morning at ten to eight.

Doorkeeper: OK, wait a few minutes, please.

(He is checking)

D: Well, according to the cctv, there was nobody in or out of your room besides you and your roommates.

G: Thank you any way.

D: That's OK. I hope it **turns up**[3].

习惯用语 3

① upside down: 翻了个底朝天，为了找某物而挪开所有的东西
② cctv: 闭路电视
③ turn up: （被）找到，（被）发现

E: 嗨 Gavin，怎么了？看上去闷闷不乐的。
G: 你看见我的 MP4 了吗？
E: 你的 MP4？你昨天没用吗？
G: 用了，但现在找不到了。我把宿舍都翻遍了，可是……
E: 你是说，肯定有人拿了你的 MP4，对吗？
G: 有可能。可是今早是我最后一个离开宿舍的。我清楚地记得我把门锁好了。而且还有两个门卫，小偷怎么可能进去呢？
E: 我不知道。让他们翻看一下闭路电视啊。也许能找到什么有用的线索。
G: 嗯！这是唯一的机会了。

(在接待处)

G: 你好，先生。我是住在 236 房间的学生，我的 MP4 不见了，我觉得可能是被人偷了。你能帮我查一下闭路电视吗？我是早上 7 点 50 分离开的。

D: 好的，请稍等。

（检查中……）

D: 监控录像没发现有人进入你的宿舍，除了你和你的室友。

G: 谢谢！

D: 不客气。希望你能找到。

Questions 3

1. Have you ever lost anything in your dorm?
2. Did you ever suspect one of your dormmates?

Chapter 7 Student Activities 学生活动

28 北京 2008 奥运会
Beijing 2008 Olympics

Background Information

About 70,000 volunteers are needed for the 2008 Beijing Olympics and 30,000 for the Paralympic Games and they will be selected in March 2008. By 7 March 2007 there were 370,372 applicants including 184,312 from Beijing's universities. Most will be chosen from Beijing universities with around 3,000 from outside Beijing.

Useful information about volunteers
- General Policy for Volunteers for the 2008 Beijing Olympic and Paralympic Games
  www.beijing2008.com/39/80/article 212038039.shtml

2008 年北京奥运会需要 70000 名志愿者，残奥会需要 30000 名志愿者，这些人将于 2008 年 3 月被选出。截止到 2007 年 3 月 7 日，共有 370372 人报名，其中有 184312 人为北京的在校大学生。大部分志愿者都会从北京的大学中挑选，另外还有 3000 个京外名额。关于志愿者的有用信息：

- 关于北京 2008 年奥运会和残奥会志愿者的基本政策。
  www.beijing2008.com/39/80/article212038039.shtml

背景信息

Dialogue 1

Delia: How's your volunteering job going?
Lucy: Great! Thanks.
D: So what do you do?
L: It's mainly paperwork and not all that exciting but at least I'm helping now and who knows what I'll be doing once the Games start!
D: How did you get the job **in the first place**①?
L: It was really tough. I had to take a written test in five different languages English, Russian, Japanese, German and Korean! What about you?
D: As you know I applied to be a media volunteer so I'm having to take some courses such as Sports Journalism.
L: Does that mean you will **get up close and personal**② with any of the athletes?
D: No. I'll probably be stuck in a glass booth somewhere!
L: Is it an interesting course?
D: Well, they just teach you the basics. I much preferred Media Operations because it gives you some idea about the Games' planning and organisation.
L: It all sounds a lot more interesting than mine.
D: At least we are both involved and one day we'll be able to tell our kids that not only were we there but that it couldn't have been so successful without us!

习惯用语 1
① in the first place: 首先，刚开始
② get up close and personal: 近距离接触

D: 你的志愿者工作怎么样了?

L: 很好!谢谢。

D: 你都做些什么?

L: 以文书工作为主,并不总是那么令人兴奋。但至少我现在是有所贡献的,而且一旦奥运会开始了,不知道我会做什么呢!

D: 你最初是怎么得到这份工作的?

L: 相当艰难!先得参加一个五种语言的笔试——英语、俄语、日语、德语、韩语。你呢?

D: 正如你所知,我申请了传媒志愿者,所以我得参加一些课程,比如体育新闻。

L: 那是不是意味着你可以近距离地接触那些参赛选手?

D: 不一定,很可能我只是站在一个玻璃隔间里。

L: 课程有意思吗?

D: 只是教一些基础知识。我更喜欢媒体运作,可以了解到一些赛事规划和组织的知识。

L: 听起来都比我的有意思。

D: 起码我们都是志愿者了,将来有一天我们可以对孩子说,我们不但曾经是一名志愿者,而且要是没有我们的贡献,奥运会就不会如此成功。

Questions 1

1. Did you have to pass any exams to become an Olympic volunteer?
2. Are you taking any special courses?

Dialogue 2

Daisy: The 2008 Olympic Games are coming nearer and nearer.

Mandy: Yes, and I'm really excited about it. How I wish I could do something for this event!

D: Don't you know that the Olympic Organizing Committee is still recruiting volunteers? The door is open to you to be part of the event.

M: But I'm only a freshman. Can I have that opportunity?

D: Of course, anyone born before June 30, 1990 is eligible.

M: But my English is still poor. I don't think I can be a good guide for foreigners.

D: Oh, come on Mandy, you should have confidence. As an English major, you have many advantages. Besides, you can practice your oral English from now on.

M: Thank you, Daisy, I will do my best. Are there any other requirements?

D: Well, volunteers must be able to serve at the Games for at least seven days.

M: That means I can't go back home, but it's worth it I think, and my parents will be proud of me.

D: I'm sure you will prove to be a valuable volunteer.

M: Why do you say that?

D: You can speak Japanese! Volunteers speaking a third language besides Chinese and English are badly needed.

M: Oh, that's great! I'd better **brush up on**[①] my Japanese as well as my English.

习惯用语 2

① brush up on: 重温自己某学科的知识,通过学习(或练习)提高

D: 2008 奥运会越来越近了。

M: 是啊,我真的很兴奋。我多么希望能为奥运做些事情啊!

D: 你不知道奥组委还在招聘志愿者吗?奥运之门为你敞开着。

M: 可我只是个大一新生。我能得到那样的机会吗?

D: 当然了,凡是 1990 年 6 月 30 日以前出生的人都可以。

M: 可我的英语不好。对外国人来说,我不会是个好向导的。

D: 哦,别这样 Mandy,你得有自信!作为英语专业的学生,你有很

多优势。而且，你可以从现在就练习口语啊。
M: 谢谢 Daisy，我会尽全力的。还有什么其它的要求吗？
D: 在赛会期间，志愿者至少要能够服务 7 天。
M: 就是说我不能回家了，但我觉得很值，我的父母也会为我感到自豪的。
D: 我确信你会成为一名优秀的志愿者的。
M: 为什么这么说？
D: 你能说日语啊！除了中文和英语之外，还能说另一种外语的志愿者相当受欢迎。
M: 噢，太棒了！那除了练习英语外，我得赶紧练练我的日语了。

Questions 2

1. Have you volunteered for the Olympics?
2. Do you have an extra language?

Dialogue 3

Grant: I've registered as a volunteer for next year's Olympics. Any advice you can give me while I wait for their answer?

Nick: Obviously you should be seeking to improve your spoken English as much as possible but I would also suggest that you learn as much as you can about Western culture.

G: But there's so much to learn! I couldn't do that!

N: Just take one country at a time. For example, perhaps most tourists will come from America so you should start there.

G: OK. What aspects of American culture should I start with?

N: Let's make a list, shall we? Let's begin with politics. Then you can divide it into sub-topics such as Democrats and Republicans.

G: OK I get the idea although I think that politics is boring. What about holidays? I know a bit about Christmas and Thanksgiving. What others are there?

N: There's Halloween which is on the 31st of October and we can't forget Valentine's Day.

G: But you forgot the fourth of July! I think those are the main ones. Another topic?

N: Social behaviour for one. How do Americans behave in a **social setting**①?

G: You mean at parties and mealtimes?

N: Yes, that sort of thing. And you could think about religion.

G: Another boring subject!

N: Maybe to some but you need to remember that belief affects behaviour. Just as China honours and respects Confucius so you should respect other people's beliefs.

G: I see I am going to be busy for the next year!

习惯用语 3

① social setting: 社会公共场合

G: 我已经报名参加明年奥运会的志愿者了。在我等待回音的这段时间，你有什么好建议吗？

N: 显然，你需要尽可能地提高你的口语水平，我还建议你尽可能地多学一点儿西方文化知识。

G: 可是要学的太多了！我都忙不过来了！

N: 一次就学一个国家。比如，许多游客可能都来自美国，你可以从那里开始着手。

G: 好。我应该从美国文化的哪一个方面开始呢？

N: 咱们来列个清单吧。从政治开始。然后你可以将其继续划分，比如民主党和共和党。

G: 好的，我明白了，虽然我觉得政治有些无聊。还有美国假日呢？我知道一些关于圣诞节和感恩节的事情。还有什么别的吗？

N: 10 月 31 号的万圣节，还有情人节。

G: 你忘了美国独立日！这是很重要的。还有什么别的话题吗？

N: 人们的社交行为，比如美国人在公共场合的行为举止。

G: 你是说在聚会和进餐的时候？

N: 对，就是那一类事情。你还可以考虑一下宗教。

G: 又是一个无聊的话题！

N: 对有些人来说是这样。但你得记住，信仰决定行为。就像中国人尊敬孔子那样，所以你也应该尊重他人的信仰。

G: 明白了。看来明年我有的忙了。

Questions 3

1. Do you know anything about Western culture?
2. Which are the main aspects of Western culture that you should know?

Chapter 8 Learning English 英语学习

29 口语
Speaking

Background Information

Most people view command of a language by how well you speak it. If you never speak then people will think you are dumb. Of the 4 key skills in learning a language; listening, speaking, reading and writing, speaking is different from the other three because speaking is the one thing you cannot do alone.

You can listen to English alone.
You can read English alone.
You can write English alone.

But you can't really speak English alone because speaking English is far better done with a partner. That is why you should make every effort possible to find someone to speak with. Your roommate, classmate or friend can be the one that you regularly speak with in English. The more often you speak in English then the more your English will improve.

许多人都把口语作为衡量语言能力的标准。要是你从来不开口说，人们会觉得你没有能力。在语言学习的四项主要技能——听、说、读、写中，"说"不同于其他三者，因为你不可能来单独完成"说"的内容。

你可以单独听英语、读英语、写英语，但却不能单独说英语，因为说英语需要一个搭档才会更有效。所以你要尽一切所能去寻找一个可以和你说英语的人，比如你的室友、同学或者朋友都可以成为你的口语搭档。英语说得越多，就越会有长进。

背景信息

Dialogue 1

Amanda: I suppose you get asked this question many times, but how can I improve my spoken English?

Nick: The main thing to remember is that you have two ears, two eyes and only one mouth so you need to increase your listening and reading before speaking.

A: But I know one famous American teacher at New Chinglish School who says that the only way to improve our speaking is by speaking.

N: Unfortunately I know him too but it's really not good advice. Think about it for a moment. If you and a classmate spoke all day to each other what would be the result at the end of the day?

A: We'd only have spoken what we already know, right?

N: Yeah, so your vocabulary hasn't increased at all. Speaking a lot is good for your confidence but you really need to increase your vocabulary which is why I suggest that you read and listen a lot.

A: And what new vocabulary we learn we should use, right?

N: Spot on![①] You also need to get feedback from who you speak with as to the correctness of the words you use.

A: Does that mean I should only talk to foreigners, then?

N: Not at all! But you should find a conversation partner whose English is a bit better than yours.

A: What else should I do while in conversation?

N: Listen intelligently to what is said, look out for interesting phrases and try to talk on one subject in as many different ways as possible.

A: Why one subject?

N: Because that forces you to use many different words to discuss one topic.

A: Great advice! Thanks Nick.

习惯用语 1

① Spot on! 正确!

A: 我想很多人都问过你这个问题了，但我还想问一下，怎么能提高我的口语？
N: 首先要记住的是，你有两只耳朵、一双眼睛，但只有一张嘴，所以你在说之前需要加强听和读的能力。
A: 但是我知道新汉英学校一个很有名的美国教师说过，提高口语的唯一方法就是说。
N: 正好我也认识他，但他的这个建议不怎么样。你好好想一想，如果你和一个同学聊了一整天，最后会是什么结果？
A: 我们只会说一些我们已经知道的，对吗？
N: 是的，所以你们的词汇量根本不会增加。多说对建立自信很有好处，但是你真的需要增加你的词汇量，这就是我为什么建议你要多读多听。
A: 另外我们应该多用我们学到的新单词，对吗？
N: 对了！在你与对方交谈的过程中，还需要从他那里得到反馈，比如说某些词你用得是否准确。
A: 那是不是说我应该只跟外国人交流？
N: 那倒也不是！但是你应该找一个英语水平略好于你的交流对象。
A: 在谈话中我还应该做些什么？
N: 在听别人说话的时候，要学得聪明点，关注一下对方谈话的内容，留心一下有意思的短语，试着用尽可能多的方式表达一个主题。
A: 为什么是一个主题？
N: 因为这就要求你用很多不同的词来讨论这个话题。
A: 好建议！谢谢 Nick。

Questions 1

1. How would you rate your spoken English? Poor, fair, average, good, excellent?
2. Do you have a conversation partner?

Dialogue 2

Daisy: I have to enter a speech contest. What advice can you give me?

Nick: You need to know the format of the speech contest first.

D: I have three minutes to prepare a speech on a topic they will give me. Then I have to speak for two minutes and then answer a question about it for one minute.

N: You should prepare a list of topics and write a short speech on each one.

D: Why write if it's for a speech?

N: All the best speeches are written first. In any case, it helps you to structure a speech correctly.

D: So what's a speech structure like?

N: It helps if you see it as comprising five parts. The first part is the introduction. The next three parts are your three main points and the final part is the conclusion.

D: Why three main points?

N: Because any less than that is too little and any more is too long! Three is an ideal number.

D: What about the introduction?

N: This is where you introduce the topic and mention your three main points. Try to start your introduction with something that will **grab the audience's attention**[①] like a statistic, a fact, a joke, a quotation or a story. But make sure it's relevant to

your topic.
D: Any other suggestions?
N: Try to modulate your voice so that sometimes you stress certain words or phrases and remember that pauses can be very effective.

习惯用语 2

① grab sb.'s attention: 抓住某人的注意力

D: 我得参加一个演讲比赛。你有什么好建议吗?
N: 你首先要了解演讲比赛的形式。
D: 在现场他们给我一个话题,我有 3 分钟的时间做准备。然后我得演讲两分钟,再用一分钟回答一个相关的问题。
N: 你应该准备一份主题清单,然后针对每个主题写一个简短的演讲稿。
D: 既然是一次演讲,为什么要写下来?
N: 所有出色的演讲都是先写出来的。无论如何,这会帮助你正确的组织一篇演讲结构。
D: 那么演讲的结构应该怎样呢?
N: 对你有帮助的结构由五部分组成。第一部分是导言。下面三部分是你所要阐述的三个要点,最后一部分是总结。
D: 为什么要三个要点?
N: 因为少了就太短,多了又太长了!三个是最理想的。
D: 导言是干什么用的?
N: 提出你的主题并提及三个要点。试着用统计数据、事实、笑话、引语或故事一类的内容开始你的导言部分,以吸引听众的注意力。但要确保和你讨论的主题相关。
D: 还有其他的建议吗?
N: 调整你的音调,以便强调某个词或短句,还要记住,停顿是非常有效的。

Questions 2

1. Have you ever entered a speech contest?
2. Do you ever practice making a speech?

Dialogue 3

Olivia: Hi! Is this your first visit to Renda's English Corner?

Nick: No, it's not. I often come here on a Friday night.

O: Judging by your accent, you must be British, right?

N: Clever girl! I actually come from Leeds which is in the north of England.

O: I also guess from your age and **smart appearance**① that you're a teacher. Am I right?

N: You certainly are! Now it's my turn. You're obviously a student but I'd **hazard a guess**② that you're not an English major, right?

O: You're right but do you say that because of my poor English?

N: No, your English is quite good. It's just that English majors don't seem interested in learning English.

O: Well, I'm interested in learning English! Have you any suggestions on how I can improve my spoken English?

N: You're obviously doing one great thing which is coming to an English Corner and conversing with a foreigner. Tonight, I'd suggest that you try to have as many short conversations with as many foreigners as possible. But make sure you talk about something different with each one.

O: Why short conversations and different topics?

N: Short because you don't want to monopolise the conversation and different topics so that you're not repeating yourself every

time.
O: Great suggestions! Thanks a lot. See you later!

习惯用语 3

① smart appearance: 穿得很精神　　② hazard a guess: 大胆地猜测

O: 嗨！你是第一次来人大英语角吗？
N: 不是。我星期五晚上经常来。
O: 从你的口音判断，你一定是英国人，对吗？
N: 聪明的女孩！实际上我来自英国北方的利兹。
O: 从你的年龄和潇洒的外表来看，我猜你是一位老师，对吗？
N: 对了！现在轮到我猜了。很显然你是个学生，但我猜你不是英语专业的，对吗？
O: 对了，你这么说，是不是因为我的英语不好？
N: 不是，你的英语很不错。这是因为英语专业的学生似乎对学习英语没什么兴趣。
O: 哦，我对学英语很有兴趣！您有什么好建议能帮我提高口语吗？
N: 你能来英语角和外国人对话显然是很正确的选择。我建议你今晚试着和尽可能多的外国人进行简短的交谈。但是确保每一次谈论的内容都不相同。
O: 为什么要进行简短的交谈还要谈不同的话题？
N: 简短是因为你不要自己不停地说而对方没有说话的机会，不同的话题以便你不用每次都重复自己上一次的话。
O: 这建议太棒了！非常感谢。再见！

Questions 3

1. Do you ever go to English Corners?
2. What are the advantages and disadvantages of English Corners?

Chapter 8 Learning English 英语学习

30 写作 Writing

Background Information

Writing, and the ability to write extensively and well, in highly developed societies, remains the prerogative of an educated minority. If you want to write well in English then you should learn to write well in Chinese as writing skills are transferable from one language to another. It is correspondingly bizarre that extensive writing in a foreign language should play anything other than a specialist role in foreign language learning.

在高度发达的现代社会中，写作能力，确切来说是能够就广泛题材写出质量上乘的作品的能力，不是普通人所能够拥有的，只有少数受过良好教育的人才能掌握。如果你想要练好英文写作，那么你应该先学好中文写作，因为不同语言之间，写作技巧是相通的。同样地，在外语教学方面，让学生进行大量外语写作训练是很重要的，如果不这样，那倒很奇怪了。

Dialogue 1

Alice: My writing is so bad! What can I do?

Nick: The best thing is to change the way that you write.

A: What do you mean by that?

N: Well, most Chinese students leave their writing until the last possible moment. Is that true of you?

A: I'm blushing. That's my answer!

N: First of all you should regard your writing as a process and not as a product.

A: Process? Product?

N: This means that you see your writing as evolving over time rather than writing something which you then see as finished. Good writing takes time.

A: I see. Tell me how it works **in practice**[①].

N: OK. Whatever you write you should regard it as a first draft. Once you finish this first draft you should use the spell check. Next you should print it out.

A: And then hand it in, right?

N: No! You should have a look at it the next day. See if you can spot any mistakes. Also read it out loud to see if it sounds OK.

A: Why the next day?

N: Because then you can **look at it afresh**[②]. You're more likely to see mistakes that way. And when you read it you should try to think about what you wrote and see if you can express it better. Only after you have done several drafts should you hand it in.

A: Thanks, Nick. I'll try it that way in future.

习惯用语 1

① in practice: 在实践中　　② look at sth. afresh: 重新看待某事

A：我的写作太差了！我该怎么办啊？
N：最好的方法是改变你写作的方式。
A：什么意思？
N：嗯，大部分中国学生一直拖到最后一刻才开始写作文。你也是吧？
A：真不好意思。我就是这样！
N：首先你应该把写作当作一个过程而不是一个结果。
A：过程？结果？
N：这就是说你要把写作当作是一个不断提炼的过程，而不是一个最终的产品。优秀的文章需要时间。
A：我明白了。那在实践中具体该怎么做呢？
N：好的。无论你写什么，你都应该把它视为最初的草稿。你完成后，检查拼写。然后把它打印出来。
A：然后交上去，对吗？
N：不是！你应该第二天再看看。看你是否可以找出一些错误。也可以大声地读出来看是否通顺。
A：为什么是第二天再看？
N：因为那时你可以重新考虑自己写的东西，更容易发现错误。当你阅读的时候你应该再好好想想你写的内容，看能否用更好的方式来表达。在你完成了几次修改之后再交上去。
A：谢谢，Nick。我以后会尝试这种方法的。

Questions 1

1. Is your writing product based or process based?
2. How much time do you spend on writing an essay?

Dialogue 2

Ivy: What's the best way of learning new words?

Nick: Well, it's certainly not by writing word lists. This is the worst possible way of learning vocabulary.

I: Why do you say that? You know that all our teachers give us lots of new words that we have to learn.

N: But you only learn those words for exams and then once the exam is over you forget them all! In fact, the brain finds it difficult to remember single words. The brain finds it far easier to remember phrases, collocations and multi-word expressions.

I: So I should throw away my word lists and replace them with lists of phrases, right?

N: Yes. Any new word that you come across you should first look for its definition and then look for words that it normally goes with. These are called collocations. For example, someone who smokes a lot is called a heavy smoker. So heavy smoker is a collocation. I suggest you buy a collocation dictionary.

I: Right, I will. Now, you mentioned phrases?

N: Yes, we use them a lot every day. Phrases like how are you? what's up? on the other hand and so on. Most teachers concentrate on single words and then try to build up a sentence word by word when it is better to use larger units or phrases.

I: Can you give me an example?

N: Take the expression "I've got a stone in my shoe." You could replace "a stone" with "a pebble", "some sand" or "something". This way you learn a general expression which you can alter accordingly.

I: That certainly sounds logical.

N: Ha! You're using a general expression there "that sounds...."

I: So I could have said "that sounds interesting" or even "that sounds stupid"!

N: Yes. You know the basic phrase and how it can be adapted according to what you want to say.

I: I think my English is really going to increase **by leaps and bounds**① now that you've told me the secret of learning English!

习惯用语2

① by leaps and bounds: 非常迅速地

I：学习新单词最好的方法是什么？

N：嗯，绝对不是用单词列表。这可能是最差的学习词汇的方法。

I：为什么这么说？你知道所有的老师都给我们很多要学的新单词。

N：但是你仅仅是为了考试学习那些词汇，一旦考试结束你就忘了！事实上，大脑很难记住独个的单词，而记住短语、词组和复合词表达就容易得多。

I：所以我应该抛开单词表，用短语列表来代替，对吗？

N：是的。遇到任何新单词，你首先应该了解它的定义，然后看它通常都和什么单词组合使用，这就叫搭配。例如，某人抽很多烟就叫他 heavy smoker（大烟鬼），heavy smoker 就是一个词组。我建议你买一本搭配词典。

I：好，我会买一本。你刚才提到了短语？

N：是的，我们每天都使用大量的短语，比如：How are you? 你好吗？What's up? 怎么了？on the other hand 另一方面等等。大部分老师关注单个单词，然后用一个一个的单词组成一句话，其实用词组或短语更好一些。

I：你能举个例子吗？

N：比如"我鞋里有个小石头。"，你可以用"小圆石头"、"一些沙子"或者"什么东西"代替"小石头"。这样你学会了一种固定的表达方式就可以进行更多的变化了。

I：听起来很有道理。

N：哈！你正使用的就是一个句式"听起来……"

I：所以我刚才也可以说"听起来很有趣"或者"听起来很蠢"！

N：是的，你知道了基本的短语，就可以根据你想说的内容进行相应的变换。

I：我想，你告诉我学习英语的秘诀以后，现在我的英语水平可以很快地提高了。

> **Questions 2**
>
> 1. What are the advantages and disadvantages of word lists?
> 2. Do you know any general expressions?

Dialogue 3

Tony: My teacher insists that all our writing is done by hand. What do you think?

Nick: I think you should get a new teacher! No serious teacher who is concerned about the writing ability of their students would ever teach writing by hand. They should be teaching digital writing.

T: Digital writing? I've never heard of that! What is it?

N: It's simply writing that is word processed. In other words, using a computer to write with.

T: I see. But we don't have computers in the classroom.

N: Most universities would have a computer lab that you could use.

T: So what's so special about digital writing?

N: It's the way we write now. Most foreign teachers would never write anything by hand so why should you? When you graduate and start work for a company all the writing that you do will be on the computer.

T: So learning to word process is good experience for the future?

N: Yes and it makes it easier for both student and teacher.

T: Why is it easier for the student?

N: Anything that you write can be emailed to the teacher who can correct it using **Track Changes**①. That way you can easily see what mistakes you have made. It's also easier for you to rewrite because you don't have to write it out again.

T: I see. And how is it easier for the teacher?

N: Most foreign teachers don't like teaching writing because of the **heavy work load**②. But by using computers the work load is considerably reduced. When students are writing in class I can go around and point out their mistakes which they can

immediately correct. Also students can correct their classmates' work.
T: That sounds a better idea. I'm going to tell my teacher to switch over to digital writing as soon as possible!

> **习惯用语 3**
> ① Track Changes: 指修改文章时，保留修改标记（你可以在工具下拉菜单中找到）
> ② heavy work load: 工作量很大

T: 我的老师坚持让我们用手写作文。你觉得怎么样？
N: 我觉得你应该换一个新老师！没有一位认真关注学生写作能力的老师会教他们用手写作。应该教他们使用电子输入。
T: 电子输入？我从没听说过！是什么？
N: 就是文字处理方法。换句话说，就是用电脑来写。
T: 我知道了。但是我们教室没有电脑。
N: 大多数大学都有一个机房，你可以用那里的电脑。
T: 那电子输入有什么特别的吗？
N: 这是我们现在所用的写作方式。大部分外教从不用手写，你为什么用呢？当你毕业在一家公司开始工作的时候，所有你需要写的都要在电脑上完成。
T: 所以学习文字处理对将来来说是很好的经验？
N: 是的，而且对学生和老师来说都会轻松一些。
T: 为什么对学生会轻松一些？
N: 你写的任何东西都可以用电子邮件发送给老师，老师可以用修订工具进行修改。用这种方式你可以直接看到你出错的地方。对你重写来说也很容易，不用再写一遍了。
T: 我知道了。那对老师来说怎么轻松了？
N: 大部分外教不喜欢教写作因为教写作的工作量很大。但使用电脑的话工作量就会大大减少。当学生在课堂上写作的时候，我可以来回走动指出他们可以及时改正的错误。学生们也可以修改他们同学的作业。

T: 听起来是个好主意。我打算告诉我的老师尽快转变使用电子输入方法!

Questions 3

1. What kind of writing do you do in class?
2. Are you familiar with Microsoft Word?

Chapter 8　Learning English　英语学习

31　Reading　阅读

Background Information

How do you improve your reading? The answer is to read more. Try to read good interesting English which is at your level of reading or just a bit higher such as modern novels, weekly newspapers such as *21st Century* and magazines like *The World of English*. Having found some good interesting reading material you then need to read intelligently. By this, I mean looking for collocations, fixed expressions and phrases that are the essentials of English. This means not concentrating on individual words but on groups of words that go together. Research shows that students who practice extensive reading naturally acquire new vocabulary without it being expressly taught. Your reading should be extensive reading and not intensive reading.

怎样才能提高你的阅读能力？答案就是多读。读一些与自己水平相当或者略高于自己水平的、有趣的英文，比如现代小说、《21世纪》周报、《英语世界》杂志。发现好的有趣的读物后，你要认真地阅读。我的意思是，在读的过程中，你要特别留意那些固定搭配、固定表达和短语，因为这些才是英语语言的重要组成部分。这就是说不要专注于单个的词，而是要关注连用在一起的词组。研究显示，经常进行泛读练习的学生可以自然而然地学会新词，而不必刻意去诵记，因而阅读应当是泛读而不是精读。

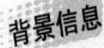
背景信息

Dialogue 1

Emma: What books do you recommend I read?
Nick: Basically anything written within the last fifty years. Before that you will find that the English will be old-fashioned and dated.
E: So that means not reading classics like Shakespeare or Austen?
N: Right, because most native speakers would find them difficult to read too. You should read modern books that are interesting.
E: How can I know whether it's interesting until I've read it?
N: If you like history then read books on history. To find out if a book is interesting or not read the **blurb**[①] on the back cover. That tells you what the book is all about.
E: But I still might not enjoy it!
N: Read page ninety-seven.
E: Why page ninety-seven?
N: Because that page will be representative of the whole. If you like that page then **the chances are**[②] you will like the book.
E: Any other advice?
N: You could find a review of that book online and that will tell you what other readers think of the book.
E: Thanks, Nick. You're a great help!

习惯用语 1
① blurb:（印在书籍护封上的）简介
② the chances are: 可能是

E: 你推荐我读什么书？
N: 基本上近 50 年出版的任何书都可以，因为你会发现在此之前的英文都是比较旧式的、过时了的英语。
E: 那就是说不要读莎士比亚或奥斯丁的那些经典的书喽？
N: 是的，因为大部分英国人都觉得那种作品很难读懂。你应该读一些有趣的现代图书。
E: 没看之前我怎么知道是不是有趣呢？
N: 如果你喜欢历史那就看一些历史书。看一下书的封底上的简介就可以知道是否有趣。它会告诉你书里都写了什么。
E: 但是我还是有可能不喜欢呢！
N: 看第 97 页。
E: 为什么是 97 页？
N: 因为那页代表整本书。如果你喜欢那页的内容那你就有可能喜欢这本书。
E: 还有别的建议吗？
N: 你可以在线找找有关这本书的书评，就能知道其他读者对这本书的看法。
E: 谢谢，Nick。你给了我很大帮助！

Questions 1
1. What books do you like to read?
2. What decides whether you buy a book or not?

Dialogue 2

Philip: How can I read faster?
Nick: Why should you read faster?
P: My teacher says that my reading speed is too slow.
N: Mine is too, sometimes! I don't really **see the point**[①] of increasing your reading rate. It's far better to concentrate on understanding what you are reading. For example, you may need to read certain parts of a textbook several times in order to fully understand it. So that means you have to read slowly.
P: What about reading novels?
N: Well, you read novels for pleasure just as you eat for pleasure. Imagine what harm you would do to your **digestive**

system② if you ate too quickly!

P: I see. In our reading class we spend a lot of time reading silently. What do you think?

N: It's a waste of time. Does you no good at all. Instead you should read out loud so that your teacher can listen to you and correct your English.

P: Correct my English in what way?

N: He should look out for pronunciation and the rhythm and stress of English.

P: What rhythm?

N: Most Chinese students make the mistake of reading each word separately and clearly and this **makes for**③ unusual sounding English!

习惯用语 2

① see the point: 了解为什么这样的原因
② digestive system: 消化系统
③ makes for: 导致

P: 我怎样才能提高阅读速度呢?

N: 干嘛要提高阅读速度?

P: 我的老师说我的阅读速度太慢了。

N: 我的阅读速度有时候也很慢!我真的不知道为什么要提高阅读速度。阅读时更应该集中注意力在理解阅读的内容上。比如,你可能需要对课本中的某些部分进行多次阅读以便全面地理解其含义。就是说你一定得慢慢读。

P: 那读小说呢?

N: 读小说是为了获得乐趣,就像吃东西一样。试想一下如果你吃得太快会给你的消化系统带来什么伤害!

P: 我知道了。在阅读课上,我们花很多时间默读。你觉得怎么样呢?

N: 浪费时间。对你根本没有帮助。你应该大声读出来以便你的老师能够听到并纠正你的英语。

P: 用什么方式纠正我的英语?

N: 他应该留心英语的发音、韵律和重音。
P: 什么韵律?
N: 大部分中国学生都会犯这样的错误,将每个词明显分开地读出来,而这导致了听起来不太自然的英语!

Questions 2

1. Do you think it is necessary to increase your reading speed? Why? Why not?
2. Do you have someone listen to you when you read out loud?

Dialogue 3

Judy: In my course I have to read many textbooks and recommended books. How can I read them more efficiently?

Nick: You should use the 80/20 principle.

J: The 80/20 principle! What's that?

N: It's a principle that can be applied to most things. For example, regarding crime, it states that 80 percent of crime is committed by 20 percent of criminals. So if you could put those criminals **behind bars**① then your crime rate would drop dramatically.

J: So how does that principle apply to reading textbooks?

N: Well, you'll probably find that 80 percent of the information you need will be found in 20 percent of the book. The key thing is knowing which 20 percent.

J: So go on, tell me!

N: The key chapters are the introduction and conclusion. Also some textbooks have a summary at the end of a chapter so you only need to read this part. Furthermore, the principle suggests, it will only take you 20 percent of the time it would normally take you, to find 80 percent of what you need.

J: Wow! You've just saved me an enormous amount of time!

N: As far as recommended books go, you should look for reviews of them in **peer-reviewed**② journals because they will not only review the book but give their strengths and weaknesses too.

J: You are amazing Nick! Thanks a lot!

习惯用语 3

① behind bars: 在监狱
② peer-reviewed: 评论，书评（被其他与文章作者资历相当的专家评论）

J: 我的专业需要阅读很多课本和参考书。我怎么能更有效地阅读呢？

N: 你应该用 80/20 定律。

J: 80/20 定律是什么？

N: 是一个可以运用到很多方面的定律。例如，关于犯罪，80% 的犯罪行为是由 20% 的罪犯犯下的。因此，如果你能够将那些惯犯关进监狱，那么犯罪率就会明显降低。

J: 那么这个定律怎么运用到读书上来呢？

N: 嗯，你可能会发现在一本书中，20% 的内容中包括了你所需要的 80% 的信息。关键是你要知道那 20% 的内容在哪里。

J: 继续，请告诉我！

N: 最关键的章节是导论和结论。一些课本的每章最后都有一个总结，所以你只需要阅读这一部分。此外，定律还表明，应该用你通常所用时间的 20%，找到你需要的 80% 内容。

J: 哇！那可以节省大量的时间！

N: 至于参考书，你可以看一些评论杂志上关于参考书的评论，他们不仅对书进行评论，而且还分析参考书的优点和缺点。

J: 你太厉害了，Nick！非常感谢！

Questions 3

1. How do you go about reading books for your course?
2. Do you ever read journals to do with your field of research?

Chapter 8 Learning English 英语学习

32 听力
Listening

Background Information

We first learn a language by listening. This is how you learnt Chinese. It is the same with English. Listening as much as possible and learning listening skills are important. If you go abroad to an English speaking country then you will need to be able to listen well because all your lectures will be in English. Studies have shown that we listen
- twice as much as we speak
- four times as much as we read
- five times as much as we write

我们学习一门语言首先就是通过听。你就是这么学会中文的。英语也一样。多听并学习听力技巧十分重要。如果你出国去一个英语国家，那你就需要很好的听力，因为所有的话都用英文表达。研究表明我们听的
- 是我们说的两倍
- 是我们读的四倍
- 是我们写的五倍

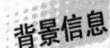
背景信息

Dialogue 1

Alison: How can I improve my listening?

Nick: There are three things to look out for when listening.

A: Just three things?

N: Yes. The first is linguistic information. These are the words that the speaker uses. Sometimes a speaker chooses some words rather than others. For example, when I am speaking to my students I may use simple words. Or when I want to stress something I may say the same thing using three different words.

A: I see. Can you give me an example?

N: You are stupid, intellectually challenged and a moron!

A: Ha ha! OK I get it. The second?

N: Paralinguistic information. This is how the words are said. There's an old saying, "it's not what you say but how you say it". The tone used, the way certain words are stressed are important clues as to the message.

A: OK. And the last one?

N: Extralinguistic information. In other words, body language. Facial expressions, body posture, hand and arm gestures are all important clues that you need to be **on the lookout for**[①].

A: So listening well does not just involve the ears but also the eyes too, right?

N: Very good Alison. You **catch on quick**[②]. I can see that you are going to make a good listener.

A: Thanks Nick.

习惯用语 1

① on the lookout for: 留心地注意着
② catch on quick: 很快地理解某事

A: 我怎么提高听力?
N: 在听的时候要留心三件事。
A: 就三件吗?
N: 是的。首先是语言信息,就是说话者用的词语。有时候一个说话者会特别选择一些单词。例如,当我跟我的学生们说话的时候我可能用一些简单的单词。当我想强调某事的时候我可能会用三个不同的词表达同一件事。
A: 我知道了。你可以给我举个例子吗?
N: 比如,愚蠢、智力上残疾的人和傻子!
A: 哈哈!好我知道了。第二件呢?
N: 超语言信息。就是如何说出这些话的。有句老话说"重要的不是你说什么而是你怎么说。"关于信息传达,使用的语调,某些词强调的方式是很重要的。
A: 好。那最后一件呢?
N: 语言之外的信息。换句话说,就是身体语言。面部表情、肢体动作、手和胳膊的姿势都是你要留心的重要方面。
A: 因此听力优秀不仅需要耳朵,还要使用眼睛,对吗?
N: 非常好 Alison。你理解得很快啊。我觉得你的听力水平很快就能提高的。
A: 谢谢 Nick。

Questions 1

1. Do you pay close attention while listening?
2. Do you notice visual clues such as body language while listening?

Dialogue 2

Glenn: What kind of listening material do you recommend?

Nick: It should be something you like. After all, they say that interest is the best teacher! And you should have a variety of tapes.

G: Does it matter if the accents are British or American?

N: Not really. It's a matter of preference. Some people like a British accent whereas others prefer an American one.

G: What if I am planning on studying in an English-speaking country?

N: Again I don't think it matters because there's no standard American or British accent. I think if you went abroad you would soon hear many different regional accents. The key thing would then be to hear as much of the **local accent**[①] as possible.

G: You said earlier about a variety of tapes.

N: Many books including this one come with MP3's. You can listen to the dialogues and imitate them. You could be one of the speakers and when it's your turn to speak you could **turn the sound down**[②].

G: Then it would be as if I was on the MP3. Cool!

N: Try listening to the news on CCTV9. This is repeated several times during the day so you can hear it more than once. And you should first listen to the news in Chinese so that you will probably know what the main headlines are.

G: That's a good idea. Any others?

N: Always try to listen to something for fun, whether it's a song or a film. But if you are watching a film make certain it has an English soundtrack and listen to it. Many students just read the Chinese subtitles and ignore what is being said. You'll never improve your English if you keep doing that!

G: I must admit that's what I do. I'll try not to do that in future.

习惯用语2

① local accent: 当地人的口音　　② turn the sound down: 调低音量

G: 你推荐哪种听力材料呢？

N: 应该是你喜欢听的内容。毕竟，兴趣才是最好的老师！你应该准备多样化的磁带。

G: 选择英音还是美音这很重要吗？

N: 这不重要，就是个人偏好的问题。一些人喜欢英音而另一些喜欢美音。

G: 如果我打算在一个英语国家学习呢？

N: 那我也觉得没什么关系，因为英音和美音没有严格的区分标准。我觉得如果你想出国，你应该尽快多听不同地区的口音。最重要的是尽可能多听当地口音。

G: 你刚才说到多样化的磁带？

N: 很多书都附带了 MP3 音频文件。你可以听对话模仿。你可以当其中一个说话者，当轮到你说的时候你就把声音关小。

G: 那就像是我在 MP3 里说话一样。真酷！

N: 试着收听中央 9 台的新闻节目。一天重播好几次，你可以不止一次的去听。但你应该先听中文新闻以便能够事先了解新闻的主要内容是什么。

G: 好主意。还有别的吗？

N: 经常找些有意思的东西来听，不管是歌曲还是电影。但是如果你看电影确保要用英文声道听。很多学生就看中文字幕而忽略了英文对白。如果你一直这样做，就永远也提高不了英语水平。

G: 我必须承认我就是这么做的。我以后尽量不这样了。

Questions 2

1. Which foreign accent do you prefer? Why?
2. How do you vary your English listening?

Dialogue 3

Diane: What can I do to make my listening more active? Sometimes I fall asleep while listening to a tape!

Nick: If all you do is listen then I'm not surprised! You should

always combine listening with doing something.
D: But do what?
N: You could repeat what has just been said. You could take notes or write a summary.
D: I do that but I find it boring.
N: Well, in that case try **interacting with**[①] the tape as much as possible. Use your imagination! Pretend that you **have a connection with**[②] the person who is speaking or with the topic.
D: Can you give me an example?
N: If it's a news item about a **car crash**[③] pretend that you are one of the relatives. Or an ambulance man called to the scene or a policeman.
D: I see. What if it's business news or something equally boring like that?
N: In that case pretend you're an investor or the CEO or just an ordinary staff member. How would that news affect your working life or finance?
D: OK I get it.
N: You could also get some of your roommates to act it out or even write your own script and record your own voices.
D: You've certainly given me some **food for thought**[④] there.

习惯用语 3

① interact with: 互动，互相影响
② have a connection with: 与…有联系
③ car crash: 汽车事故
④ food for thought: 思考素材，使某人认真思考某事

D: 怎么做我才能积极的练习听力呢？有时候听着磁带我就睡着了！
N: 如果你只是在听，那我一点儿都不惊讶！你应该在听的时候结合

着做一些别的事情。
D: 但是做什么呢?
N: 你可以复述刚刚播放的内容。还可以做记录或者写个内容摘要。
D: 我做了可是我觉得很乏味。
N: 嗯,如果那样的话就尽可能地跟磁带互动一下。运用你的想象力!假设你和正在说话的人或者话题有关系。
D: 能举个例子吗?
N: 如果是一条车祸新闻,就假设你是一位家属,或者一名被派至现场的急救人员,或者一名警察。
D: 我知道了。如果是经济新闻或其他一些类似的令人乏味的新闻呢?
N: 如果那样的话就假设你是一位投资者或者首席执行官或者仅仅是一名普通员工。这则新闻如何影响你的工作生活或财政方面?
D: 好,我明白了。
N: 你也可以叫几个室友一起把对话表演出来,或者甚至可以写出你们自己的剧本并录音。
D: 你这番话确实给了我很大启发。

Questions 3

1. What do you do to make your listening more interesting?
2. What kind of listening material do you like to listen to? Why?

Chapter 9　Finance 金融财务

33　预算管理
Managing on a Budget

Background Information

The average university student spends 537 yuan a month. A 2006 survey by Beijing Jiaotong University shows that
- 53 percent spend 200 to 600 a month
- 34 percent spend 600 to 1,000 a month
- 7 percent spend below 200 a month
- 6 percent spend more than 1,000 a month

The Internet costs 64.5 yuan a month on average.

每位大学生的平均月开销为537元。根据2006年北京交通大学的调查显示：
- 53%的学生月开销在200元至600元之间
- 34%的学生月开销在600元至1000元之间
- 7%的学生月开销低于200元
- 6%的学生月开销高于1000元

其中，平均每月的上网费是64.5元。

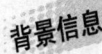
背景信息

Dialogue 1

Carl: My parents give me 600 every month for my living costs in university, I think that is not enough.

Gordon: Well my parents give me 580 and I have 50 left each month.

C: Oh, how do you manage that?

G: I spend my money only on **the bare necessities of life**①.

C: Well, I felt that everything I bought was necessary at the time. But after a few days, I felt it's not so necessary, and yet I would still repeat my behaviour.

G: Yes, you are the same as I was before.

C: Then how did you change?

G: I made a list in a notebook, writing down everything that I bought and the price. And now it's become **second nature**② to me.

C: Does it help?

G: Sure, every night before I sleep, I check my list and see which is necessary and which is not. And in the meantime, I keep my expenses within 19 per day since my parents give me 580 per month. So if I spent 21 yesterday, I would not spend more than 17 today.

C: But how did you have 50 left each month?

G: Well, if you begin to do it like this, you will spend your money very carefully, just like a miser. Sometimes I only spent 10 every day. Slowly, you will learn to **master money**③ rather than being its servant.

C: OK, I will try your way from tomorrow.

G: Why not from today?

习惯用语 1

① the bare necessities of life: 生活必需品
② second nature: 习惯，第二天性
③ master money: 理财，掌管好自己的钱财

C: 我父母每个月给我 600 块钱作为在学校的生活费，我觉得不太够啊。

G: 我父母每个月才给我 580 块，我还能剩 50 呢。

C: 噢！你是怎么省下来的啊？

G: 我只把钱花在生活必需品上。

C: 我觉得我买那些东西的时候对我来说都是必需的。可没过几天，就觉得没什么用了，但却老犯这种错误。

G: 嗯，你跟我原来的毛病一样。

C: 那你是怎么改过来的？

G: 我在笔记本上列了个清单，把我买的东西和价格都写在上面。现在这已经成为一种习惯了。

C: 有效吗？

G: 当然了。每天晚上睡觉之前，我都会检查一下清单，看看哪些是必要的，哪些不是。同时，我把每天的花销控制在 19 块钱以内，因为我父母每个月只给我 580 块。如果有一天我花了 21 块钱，那么必然有一天我的花销不能超过 17 块钱。

C: 可你每个月怎么还会有 50 块钱剩余啊？

G: 嗯，要是你也像我这样做的话，你花钱也会很小心，就跟个吝啬鬼一样。有时候我一天只花 10 块钱。慢慢的你就会学着去管理钱财，而不是成为钱财的奴隶。

C: 好的，我明天就试试你的方法。

G: 干嘛不从今天开始啊？

Questions 1

1. Do you think your parents give you enough money?
2. Do you have a budget?

Dialogue 2

Nikki: How's your finance class going?

Alyssa: It's very interesting. It's really worth spending time on. And I strongly recommend you to go with me this evening.

N: No, I don't intend to work as an accountant in the future, so it won't be of any use to me.

A: I'm not going to be an accountant, either. The finance class is not only for the students who want to work in finance but also helpful for all students.

N: Oh, the teacher will teach you how to manage a company's account, won't she?

A: Not so boring, she will teach us how to manage our income.

N: You mean, whatever the source or amount?

A: Yes, she teaches us the basic principles of maximising our income and minimising our outflow. We should have a budget and then we can work out our **disposable income**[①] so that it can be invested wisely.

N: But we don't have money to invest now.

A: That's where you're wrong! She says that if we get into the habit of saving ten percent of our income now then we'll be able to continue after graduation.

N: Maybe you are right. Every time when I think of saving money to buy a house and a car in the future, I feel hopeless. I even feel I can never make enough money to buy them.

A: Well, if you have good habits to manage your money now, I am sure you will realize your dream even before you are thirty.

N: Really?

A: I can't give you a guarantee now, but it's worth a try.

N: Then I have to go to the finance class this evening.

习惯用语 2

① disposable income: 可支配的收入（在支付了所有必要账单后，仍然剩余的钱）

N: 你那个金融课听得怎么样？
A: 特有意思。很值得花时间去听一听。我强烈建议你今晚跟我一起去听。
N: 不，我没打算将来去当会计，所以这课对我来说一点儿用都没有。
A: 我将来也不想当会计，但我还是去听，因为这个金融课不仅仅是为那些想在金融领域工作的学生准备的，对所有的学生来说都很有用。
N: 噢，老师会讲如何管理公司账户，对吗？
A: 没那么无聊。她会教我们如何管理自己的收入。
N: 你是说，不论收入的来源和数额？
A: 是的，她教给我们使收入最大化，开销最小化的基本原则。我们应该做一个预算，那样我们就可以计算出可自由支配的收入，然后用它去投资。
N: 可我们现在没有钱去投资啊。
A: 这你可错了！老师说要是我们从现在开始养成积攒 10% 收入的习惯，那么将来毕业了也会坚持下去的。
N: 也许你是对的。每次我一想到攒钱将来买车买房，就觉得希望很渺茫。我觉得永远也挣不来足够的钱去买。
A: 如果你从现在开始就养成管理财产的好习惯，我保证你的梦想会在 30 岁前实现的。
N: 真的吗？
A: 我不能保证，但这值得一试。
N: 那我今晚得跟你去听听那个金融课。

Questions 2

1. Do you think a finance class is helpful for you to manage money?
2. Did you ever think how to manage your money in the future?

Dialogue 3

Eric: It's dinner time; let's go to the dining hall together.

Paul: No thanks, I have some **instant noodles**① here.

E: Come on, you have eaten noodles for the last two days. You're becoming **as thin as a rake**②.

P: Oh, you don't understand. I want to buy a new mobile phone next year, and my parents refuse to give me money for that. So I **have no choice but to economise**③ as much as possible.

E: I think you are really stupid. Once you have bought your new mobile phone you will only use it to call the hospital.

P: Why?

E: Because you will be too weak to walk anymore!

P: Then can you find a solution for me?

E: Well, first of all, I don't think you need a new mobile phone, the one you have is still working, although it's a little bit old fashioned.

P: My friends laugh at me when they see my mobile phone.

E: OK, you can buy a new one, but you don't have to reduce your **standard of living**④ if you manage your expenses well.

P: But how?

E: Stop buying DVD games, then you will have more spare money. And once you don't play computer games anymore, you will have more spare time. So you can find a part-time job teaching computing to the freshmen or high school students. This will help you to increase your income.

P: Sounds reasonable. What should I do first?

E: Have dinner and keep in good health so that you will be able to do all that.

习惯用语 3

① instant noodles: 方便面
② as thin as a rake: 瘦得像柴耙，骨瘦如柴
③ have no choice but to economise: 除了节省别无选择
④ standard of living: 生活水平，生活标准

E: 该吃饭了,咱们一起去食堂吧。
P: 不,谢谢。我吃方便面。
E: 别啊!你都连着吃两天了,人都瘦成皮包骨了。
P: 唉,你不明白。我打算明年买个新手机,可我父母不给我钱。所以我现在别无选择,只有节衣缩食了。
E: 你可真是太愚蠢了!等你买了那个新手机,你就只能用它给医院打电话了。
P: 为什么?
E: 因为到时候你就虚弱得走不动路了。
P: 那你能帮我想出什么别的办法吗?
E: 首先,我觉得你根本不需要买新手机,你现在的这个手机虽说有点儿过时了,但是还能用啊。
P: 可我的朋友们看到我用那个手机都笑话我。
E: 那好吧,你可以买个新的,但要是你能够管理好你的开销,你完全不必降低生活水平。
P: 可是该怎么办呢?
E: 别买 DVD 游戏,那样你就会有更多剩余的钱。一旦你不玩儿电脑游戏了,你就会有更多的空余时间。这样,你可以找个兼职,教一年级新生或高中生使用电脑。这会帮你创收的。
P: 听起来挺有道理。首先我应该做什么?
E: 吃饭,保持良好的身体,以便去做之后的事情。

Questions 3

1. Do you ever spend as little as possible on food?
2. Do you use your spare time wisely?

Chapter 9　Finance 金融财务

34　银行和信用卡
Banks and Credit Cards

Background Information

Students can get loans from banks which are interest-free during their university years. They must be repaid within six years after graduation. An applicant has to submit documents, such as family income. The university may also be asked to provide proof. Visit www.csa.cee.edu.cn for more details. A national survey showed that nearly 20 percent of borrowers fail to repay their loans largely because of the difficult job market, high mobility and low awareness of a good credit rating.

学生可以从银行获得在校期间免息的银行贷款,但必须在毕业后6年内还清。申请者需要上交一些材料,例如家庭收入证明。学校也可能被要求出具相关证明。想要了解更多信息,可以浏览www.csa.cee.edu.cn。国家的一项调查表明,由于就业困难,流动性大,以及对良好信用度的观念淡薄,导致了将近20%的贷款学生在毕业后没能还清贷款。

背景信息

Dialogue 1

Hazel: Wow ... you have so much cash. Aren't you afraid of being robbed?

Jennifer: I have no choice; I don't want to go to the bank every time, that's why I take cash with me.

H: Well, I know there's often a long queue and sometimes the bank staff are rude but some are OK. And you can apply for a credit or debit card and use it in an ATM. In this way, you don't have to deal with the bank staff.

J: Yes, I'm really tired of dealing with them. When I take out a small amount of money, they look so impatient. And sometimes the ATM has problems too.

H: What problems?

J: Sometimes it **eats my card**①.

H: That's because you forgot your password I guess.

J: I read in the newspaper that people can steal your card's number and **pin number**② by using a camera fixed on the ATM.

H: That's very rare, I think.

J: You know last time when I **withdrew money**③ at an ATM, I took out some money but forgot to take my card. Someone stole my money after that. When I came back to that ATM, there was nobody there, and when I checked my account, I'd lost 1,000.

H: That's also your fault. You forgot to take your card out, so that others can still operate that ATM by using your card. Not every one is as honest as me.

J: Yes, I know. So from then on, I am really afraid to use a card.

H: But I guess you should be more careful with your cash.

习惯用语 1

① eat sb.'s card: 取款机吞卡
② pin number: 个人身份验证码
③ withdrew money: 取款

H: 哇！你有这么多现金！你就不怕被抢吗？
J: 我别无选择啊，我不想每次都去银行，所以才带这么多现金。
H: 嗯，我知道，银行老得排大队，而且有些银行职员的态度特别恶劣，有些就还不错。你可以办一张信用卡或者借记卡，在自动取款机上使用。这样就不用再跟银行职员打交道了。
J: 是啊，我真的不想再跟他们打交道了。要是我取钱数额不多，他们就显得特别不耐烦。不过有时候自动取款机也会出问题。
H: 什么问题？
J: 有时候会吞卡啊。
H: 我估计那是因为你忘了密码吧。
J: 我看报纸上说，别人可以在自动取款机上安装摄像头，偷走你的卡号和验证码。
H: 那很少见我觉得。
J: 上次我在自动取款机上取钱，把钱拿走后却忘记取卡了。然后我的钱就被偷了。我返回那台取款机时已经没人了，然后我检查账户，发现少了1000块钱。
H: 那也是你的错啊。你没有取卡，别人就可以继续在那台机器上用你的卡进行操作。不是所有人都像我这样诚实的。
J: 是的，我知道，从那以后，我就特别害怕用卡。
H: 我觉得你应该更加注意你的这些现金。

Questions 1

1. Do you prefer to keep your money in cash or at the bank?
2. Which is the best bank for students?

Dialogue 2

Kate: There are so many banks offering credit cards on campus today. Have you seen their stalls? They're giving away free gifts if you **sign up**① with them.

Philippa: Yes. But I've already got one. Mine's a Mudan student card from the Industrial and Commercial Bank.

K: I don't think we need a credit card since we don't have many chances to shop abroad and usually we won't spend more than we have.

P: Well, that is why you are **behind the times**②. In fact, the banks are helping us to accept the concept to use credit cards now. In the future, we will be a **cashless society**③, and people will also **feel free to**④ borrow money from the bank and enjoy life even when they don't have enough money at present.

K: You mean buy now, pay later! I think it was Shakespeare who said, "**Neither a borrower or a lender be**⑤."

P: Well, one reason you borrow money from a bank is to establish your **credit rating**⑥. The more you borrow and pay back on time, the higher your credit rating. Maybe one day you want to start a business, the bank will be glad to lend money to you. Because you have a good record.

K: But I don't want to borrow or spend a lot of money now.

P: It doesn't matter. You can spend a little and borrow a little. Since this credit card is especially for students, the banks charge us very little.

K: I see. Seems it's a really good deal for students.

P: Yes. And you can also use it to shop online on a foreign web site, if you don't go abroad.

K: Which would you recommend?

P: I've heard that the Young card from China Merchants Bank is quite good.

K: Then I will apply for one tomorrow.

习惯用语 2

① sign up: 在银行开户
② behind the times: 落后于时代，过时
③ cashless society: 无纸币时代
④ feel free to: 能够做某事
⑤ Neither a borrower or a lender be: 既不借钱给别人，也不向别人借钱
⑥ credit rating: 信用等级

K: 今天有好多家银行都在学校里办理信用卡。你看见他们的摊位了吗？申请开户就免费送礼物。

P: 嗯，我申请了一个，是工商银行的牡丹学生卡。

K: 我觉得我们不需要信用卡，因为我没有太多机会去境外购物，而且，通常我们也不会超出自己的能力来消费。

P: 哈，所以你才落伍了。其实银行是在帮助我们接受使用信用卡的理念。将来会是一个无纸化货币的时代，人们可以从银行借款，即使当前没有足够的现金也可以享受生活。

K: 你是说先消费，后还款！我记得莎士比亚说过，"不要借钱给别人，也不要向别人借钱。"

P: 你向银行借款的原因之一就是建立自己的信用等级。你借得越多，且准时还款，你的信用级别就会越高。也许有一天，当你想要开办公司的时候，鉴于你的良好信用记录，银行会很乐意借钱给你。

K: 可我现在不想借入或花费太多钱。

P: 没关系。你可以少花少借。这个信用卡是专门为学生设计的，银行的收费也很低。

K: 我明白了。似乎是个好东西。

P: 是啊，要是你不出国的话，你还可以用它在国外的网站上在线购物。

K: 你推荐哪种卡？

P: 我听说招商银行的青年卡很不错。

K: 那我明天就去申请一个。

Questions 2

1. Do you have a credit card?
2. What are the advantages and disadvantages?

Dialogue 3

Bob: Where are you going?

Henry: Off to the bank to pay some bills.

B: That's so old-fashioned! You should get an online bank account like mine.

H: No way! I've heard all kinds of bad things about them.

B: Such as?

H: It's too easy for fraudsters to get your details and then **clean out**① your account.

B: Come on! The banks wouldn't be offering such services if they didn't have the security measures to deal with them.

H: I've heard about **trojan software**② that records every keystroke you make on your computer and that way they can get your **bank access codes**③.

B: That's not very likely to happen.

H: Whether it's likely or not I'm sticking to high street banking.

B: Just think of all those queues and the time you have to spend waiting.

H: At least my money is safe.

B: You go your way and I'll go mine④**!**

习惯用语 3

① clean out: 清空
② trojan software: 木马病毒软件（隐藏在其它软件中的一种病毒软件）
③ bank access codes: 进入银行账户的密码
④ You go your way and I'll go mine: 各走各的路，分道扬镳

B: 你去哪儿？
H: 去银行付账单。
B: 真跟不上时代！你应该跟我一样办个网上银行账户。

H: 我可不。我听说了很多关于网上银行的负面消息。
B: 比如呢？
H: 你的详细信息很容易泄漏，然后你的账户就被一扫而空。
B: 得了！银行要是没有处理这些安全问题的措施就不会提供这种服务了。
H: 我听说过一种木马病毒软件，它可以复制出敲击键盘的纪录，从而得到你的银行口令密码。
B: 这种事儿很少发生。
H: 不管它是否可能发生，我还是坚持去马路边上的银行办理业务。
B: 那你也不想想银行里那排大队和你花费的等待时间。
H: 至少我的钱是安全的。
B: 那行吧，咱们各走各的道儿。

Questions 3

1. Would you ever open an online bank account?
2. What are the advantages and disadvantages of online banking?

Chapter 9 Finance 金融财务

35 奖学金
Scholarships

Background Information

Most universities offer scholarships. If you work hard and have good scores, you can qualify. Academic scholarships are usually awarded yearly and do not often apply to freshmen, because they do not have an academic record. But they can be obtained during the second year if a student does well in class. There are government programmes such as the People's Scholarship and grant giving bodies such as China Foundation for Poverty Alleviation (www.fupin.org.cn) and China Youth Development Foundation (www.cydf.org.cn). There are also private ones such as the China Soong Ching Ling Foundation Future Project (www.sclf.org).

大部分大学都会提供奖学金。只要你学习努力且成绩优异,就符合申请奖学金的要求。学科奖学金通常每年颁发一次,且不会颁给大一新生,因为他们还没有学习成绩记录。但如果他们表现良好,等到二年级的时候就可以获得学科奖学金。还有一些政府项目奖学金,比如人民奖学金,其发放主体为中国扶贫基金会和中国青少年发展基金会。也有私人奖学金,比如中国宋庆龄基金会"未来工程"。

背景信息

Dialogue 1

Benson: Thomas will treat us to a dinner tonight, will you go?
Neil: Thomas? Are you serious?
B: Yes, he is one of the 10 students who got the scholarship provided by our department.
N: I see. I think he just wants **to show off**[①].
B: No, I think he is sincere. He said he wanted to thank us for our friendship. And he studied really hard.
N: OK, I will go. But I don't think the way to judge who can get a scholarship is not fair sometimes. I study hard too. It's only because he is a little bit luckier than me.
B: Of course, we know you studied hard, and everyone deserves a bit of luck. But scholarships are there to encourage us. I don't think anyone is studying just to get one.
N: But some people still think the students who get a scholarship are better than the students who didn't get one.
B: Maybe, but not me. Although he is doing better than you in our department, I am not sure he will do better than you in the future.
N: You are trying to comfort me, aren't you?
B: No, it's true. And this is only the first year; we still have another three years to go. Who knows what will happen next year?
N: Yes, I agree with you. I will study harder next year.
B: I am sure you will get a scholarship sooner or later.

习惯用语 1

① to show off: 炫耀

B: Thomas 今晚请客吃饭，你去吗？
N: Thomas？你没开玩笑吧？
B: 没错。他得到系里的奖学金了，总共就十个人。
N: 噢，我觉得他只是想炫耀一下。
B: 没有，我觉得他挺诚恳的。他说是为了我们之间的友谊而请客的，再说他平时学习真挺刻苦的。
N: 好吧，我去。但我觉得有时候奖学金的评定方式不是很公平。我学习也很刻苦啊。只不过他比我幸运点儿罢了。
B: 当然，我们知道你学习很努力。每个人都需要一点儿运气。奖学金只是为了鼓励我们，没有谁刻苦学习只是为了得奖学金。
N: 但好多人还是觉得那些得到奖学金的学生比没有得到的优秀。
B: 也许吧，但我不这样认为。虽然他现在在系里比你表现得好一点儿，但我不能确定他将来仍然比你优秀。
N: 你在安慰我，是不是？
B: 没有，这是事实。这只是第一年，我们还有三年呢。谁知道明年会发生什么啊？
N: 嗯，我同意。明年我得更加努力。
B: 我确定你迟早会得到奖学金的。

Questions 1

1. Have you ever won any scholarships before?
2. Do you think the students who get a scholarship are doing better than the students who don't?

Dialogue 2

Jessica: If, **by some strange fluke**[①], you've ever got a scholarship, what would you do with it?

Alice: What do you mean fluke! If I got one it would be because of my hard work!

J: Hah! So why haven't you got one yet?

A: You know there's a lot of competition for them.

J: Come on! Answer my question!

A: Well, it depends on how much it was.

J: Let's suppose it's 500.

A: OK, I think I will buy a heater for my mother to use in winter.

J: Oh, you are so boring? You know parents never care about things like that. If you buy it, they will think you are wasting money.

A: What would you do?

J: I think I will buy a MP3 to study English.

A: Come on, I think you only want to listen to music.

J: Well, sometimes but mainly for study.

A: I still think I will buy something for my parents. After all, they are working hard to support me here in university.

J: But I think it's better to buy something that can help you study and make more progress in your English.

A: Yes, you're right. Then I will spend 200 to buy a collocation dictionary and 300 to buy a heater for my mother.

习惯用语2

① by some strange fluke: 侥幸，偶然

J: 要是你侥幸得到了奖学金，你会用它来干什么？

A: 什么叫侥幸啊！就算我得到了奖学金，也是凭自己的努力啊！

J: 哈！那你为什么还得不到呢？

A: 你知道竞争是很激烈的。

J: 快点，回答我的问题！

A: 那得看有多少钱。

J: 假设是500块。

A: 嗯，那我会给我妈妈买个冬天用的电暖器。
J: 噢，也太没创意了吧？你明知道做父母的从不会在意那些东西。要是你买了，他们也会觉得你是在浪费钱。
A: 换作你呢？
J: 我会买一个MP3，学英语用。
A: 得了，你只是想用来听音乐罢了。
J: 有时候听音乐，但主要还是学英语用。
A: 我还是觉得我会给父母买些东西。毕竟他们辛辛苦苦地供我上大学。
J: 但我觉得买一些对你学习有帮助的东西会更好一些，让你的英语更上一层楼。
A: 对，你说得没错。那我就花200元买本搭配字典，再花300元给我妈买个电暖器。

Questions 2

1. If you get a scholarship, what would you do with it?
2. Will you buy anything for your parents out of your scholarship?

Dialogue 3

Diana: Mum[①], as today is Mother's Day I have a gift for you.
Mum: Oh, what's that?
 D: You guess.
 M: Some cosmetics?
 D: No, I think your face doesn't need make up.
 M: Then a handbag?
 D: No, in fact it is not something useful.
 M: So, you want to help me with the housework?
 D: No, better than that.
 M: Come on! Tell me what you've got for me?
 D: OK. Close your eyes and open your hands.

M: It feels very light. It's a letter, isn't it?
D: Yes. You can open your eyes and open it now.
M: It's from your university. You haven't been in trouble again?
D: No! It's good news, not bad news.
M: Wah! You've got a scholarship.
D: And not just an ordinary scholarship but a first class one.
M: Let me see. Oh, yes that's true. You may have my looks but I'm glad you've got your father's brains.
D: I told you not to worry about my study.

习惯用语 3

① Mum: 英式英语（Mom 是美式英语）

D: 妈妈，今天是母亲节，我给你买了个礼物。
M: 噢？是什么？
D: 你猜。
M: 化妆品？
D: 不是，你的脸不需要那些东西。
M: 那，手提包？
D: 不是，其实是个没什么大用的礼物。
M: 那，你想帮我做家务？
D: 不是，比那个要好。
M: 快点，告诉我你到底买了什么？
D: 好，闭上眼，伸出双手。
M: 我觉得很轻，是一封信，对吗？
D: 是的，现在你可以睁开眼睛，打开信看一看。
M: 从你大学寄来的。不会是你又惹什么麻烦了吧？
D: 没有！是个好消息，不是坏消息。
M: 哇！你得到奖学金了！
D: 而且不是一般的奖学金，是一等奖学金。

M: 我看看。嗯，没错。你长得像我，但却遗传了你爸爸的聪明脑袋。

D: 我早就跟你说了不用担心我的学习。

Questions 3

1. How would you tell your parents that you had just won a scholarship?
2. Do you take after your mother or father?

Chapter 9 Finance 金融财务

36 股票市场
The Stock Market

Background Information

In the past one and a half years the Chinese stock market has boomed and the Shanghai Composite Index broke through the 4,000 barrier shortly after the 2007 May holidays. Share prices have risen by 50 percent this year following a 130 percent gain in 2006. Some analysts predict that the 5,000 barrier will be broken soon. As a result some 7 percent of Chinese are investing in stocks. Some authorities have suggested that interuniversity stock investment contests should be stopped because they may encourage students to invest on the stock market.

在过去一年半的时间里，中国的股市快速上涨。2007年五一假期刚过，上证指数就突破了4000点大关。继2006年股价大涨了130%之后，今年股价又上升了50%。一些分析家预言，5000点大关很快就会冲破。因此，7%的中国人投入到了股市当中。权威人士称，大学里的模拟股市投资竞赛应该终止，因为这会促使学生们投入股票市场。

背景信息

Dialogue 1

Malcolm: The stock market is really hot now. I'm thinking of getting into it.

Casey: Well, I suggest you be careful. It's easy to **get your fingers burnt**①.

M: My uncle works for a securities company. He will help me to make an **investment portfolio**②.

C: But I think the hotter the market is, the more risk there is.

M: Yes, you are right. But the more risk there is, the more profit there might be.

C: I do hope you can win but what if you lose?

M: Well, that's life. My uncle says the stock market is like life. Sometimes you are up; sometimes you are down. You have no choice but to take life as it is.

C: Do you really have **such a couldn't care less attitude**③? It's easier said than done.

M: Maybe, but I'll try. In fact, I don't care about how much money I can make. I just want to widen my knowledge on finance and gain more experience of life. If I can make money, fine. I will still do what I should do in university. If I lose money, I will take it easy and forget it.

C: I wish I could be so carefree about money! But where do you get your capital from?

M: My parents support me.

C: If you lose, what will your parents do?

M: Don't worry, this is what they have earned from the stock market. They said this is for me to play with. My losing or winning will not bother them so long as I learn from it.

习惯用语 1

① get sb.'s fingers burnt: 因投机买卖而亏本
② investment portfolio: 证券投资组合
③ such a couldn't care less attitude: 抱着一种根本就不在乎的态度

M: 现在股市可真火啊！我也想投入其中。
C: 我建议你小心。投机很容易使你损失惨重的。
M: 我叔叔在一家证券公司工作，他会帮我掌握好证券投资组合的。
C: 但我觉得市场越火，风险就越大。
M: 是，你说得没错。但风险越大，收益可能也会越大。
C: 我很希望你能赚钱，但要是赔了怎么办？
M: 这就是生活啊。我叔叔说股市就像人生，有起有落。你无从选择，只有服从命运的安排。
C: 你真的有这种毫不在乎的态度吗？说起来容易做起来难啊。
M: 也许吧，但我要试试。其实我不太在乎到底可以赚多少钱。我只是想扩展自己在金融方面的知识，丰富自己的人生经验。要是能赚钱，当然最好，我还是会做在学校应该做的事情；要是赔钱了，那就泰然处之，忘掉就是了。
C: 我真希望我能对金钱如此毫不在乎。可你从哪儿得到本钱呢？
M: 我父母支持我。
C: 要是你赔了，你父母会怎样？
M: 不用急，都是他们从股市赚的钱。他们说这是供我练习用的。只要我能从中学到东西，输赢无所谓。

Questions 1

1. Do ever get into the stock market?
2. Do you think it's good or bad for students to buy stocks?

Dialogue 2

Shane: How are your stocks doing?

Damien: Not at all. I sold out just after Spring Festival. What about you?

S: I'm **making a killing**①! With a **bull market**② like this it's easy to make a lot of money. Why don't you come back?

D: I'm afraid that the market's reached its limit and will start to drop from now on.

S: No way, man! There's still a long way to go.
D: I heard that the government might intervene because it's getting out of control.
S: Just rumours, man. You can't believe everything you read.
D: It's just too risky. I made a little bit of money before but I can't afford to lose it.
S: Why don't you put your money into safe stocks like the banks or China Mobile?
D: I guess I can do that but they're just for old people who don't want to risk their pensions.
S: That's for sure! I go for the high risk shares because that's where the money is.
D: You could lose all your money that way.
S: No man! I spread the risk around. I might lose a little but I gain more!
D: Well good luck. I think you'll need it!

习惯用语 2

① making a killing: 赚很多钱
② bull market: 牛市，行情看涨的市场

S: 你的股票最近如何？
D: 没了，春节一过我就全都卖了。你的呢？
S: 我赚了不少！像这样的牛市，很容易就赚很多钱。你干嘛不杀回来啊？
D: 我担心市场已经见顶了，可能就此开始下跌。
S: 不会的，老兄！还有很大的上涨空间呢。
D: 我听说政府可能会出手干预股市，因为它已经失去控制了。
S: 纯属谣言。不能随便相信。
D: 风险太高了。我之前赚了点儿钱，可是禁不起赔钱啊。
S: 你干嘛不用钱去买一些稳健的股票啊，比如银行股或者中国移动？
D: 我可以买，但我觉得那些股票都是给那些不想用养老金冒风险的老年人准备的。

S: 那倒也是！我一般都买高风险的股票，那样才能赚钱。
D: 那样你也会赔掉所有的钱。
S: 不会的！我分散风险。也许会输一点儿，但赚得更多。
D: 祝你好运，这正是你需要的。

Questions 2

1. Would you invest in safe stocks or high risk stocks? Why?
2. Are stocks just another form of gambling?

Dialogue 3

Tim: I hear everyone's getting into the stock market these days. What about you?

Heather: Well, I went along to a securities office but it was full of elderly people investing their pensions. They seem to spend all day there so it **put me off**①.

T: You should go online for all your transactions. Not only is it easier but it's quicker too. That way you don't lose any time when prices are rising or falling come to think of it.

H: But if I go online then I have to spend a lot of time in front of the computer!

T: Well, yes but it's worth it. I've already made enough this year to pay all my tuition fees and living expenses for the next two years!

H: But is that a **paper profit**②?

T: So far yes but I'll **cash some shares**③ in soon. So are you going to join in?

H: No. I prefer to do my investment using simulation. It's a virtual stock market without the risks.

T: That's just for wimps. It's not the real thing!

H: Maybe so but at least I'm getting some experience.

T: But it's not real experience! There's nothing like sitting in

front of the computer watching the latest share movements and having to **make snap decisions**④ that could make or break you.
H: I don't think my heart can take all that excitement!
T: I guess I just like the **buzz**⑤ I get.

> 习惯用语 3
>
> ① put sb. off: 使某人打消，使某人对…失去兴趣
> ② paper profit: 纸上（账面）利润，并没有真正实现的利润
> ③ cash some shares: 出卖股份，换取现金
> ④ make snap decisions: 迅速做决定
> ⑤ buzz: 兴奋，陶醉感

T: 我听说最近大家都在炒股，你呢？
H: 我也去证券营业部了，里面全都是用养老金投资的老年人，在那儿一待就是一整天。我看着就够了。
T: 你应该上网进行交易。简便又快捷。想想看，这样无论股票涨跌，你都不会延误时机。
H: 但我要是上网交易的话，就得花很多时间坐在电脑前面。
T: 是，但值得啊。我都已经赚够今年的学费和后两年的生活费了。
H: 但那不都是纸上利润吗？
T: 到目前为止是这样的，但我很快就会将其中一部分股票变现。你要不要加入？
H: 不，我更喜欢做没有风险的虚拟投资。
T: 虚拟投资都是给胆小鬼准备的，不是真东西！
H: 也许是，但至少我得到了一些经验。
T: 那并不是真正的经验！没有什么比坐在电脑前，盯着股价波动，然后迅速做出决策更有成就感的事情了！
H: 我觉得我的心脏承受不了这些刺激！
T: 我觉得自己很享受这种快感。

> Questions 3
>
> 1. Do you prefer dealing on the real or virtual stock market?
> 2. Does playing the stock market give you a buzz?

Chapter 10 Career 事业

37 实习
Internships

Background Information

An internship is any official or formal programme to provide practical experience for beginners in an occupation or profession. It may be paid or unpaid. A good site for internships is www.hiall.com.cn.

实习,就是为初学者提供的、在某一个职业领域的工作实践机会。可能有薪水也可能没有。www.hiall.com.cn 是一个比较好的实习网站。

背景信息

Dialogue 1

Rick: Hi, I'm a university student interested in internships and I was told that you're the best person to ask about **the legalities**①.

Professor Zhang: Well, I am a law professor here at Renmin University so I know a little about it. What would you like to know?

R: My first question is am I entitled to be paid?

P: Legally no according to the labour law. Students are treated as a special group and their work is not considered real employment. This means that they are not covered by the **minimum wage**② and have no insurance. So you may find some companies won't pay you at all or will only pay you for lunch and transportation.

R: That seems like cheap labour to me. Why won't they pay?

P: Well, some companies see it as providing software and hardware for students to practice what they have learned from their textbooks but they're just using their resources and not really contributing anything.

R: I can see the benefits for students getting practical experience but I still think they should get paid.

P: I think the best thing is to find out before you start whether or not you will get paid. Then you need to make a decision. After all, you will gain valuable experience and you might be offered a job too.

R: What happens if I take a paid internship and then the company refuses to pay me?

P: Unless you have a contract or **written evidence**③ then it may be difficult to prove in court. I know a student at Zhejiang University recently sued a company for not paying him for an

internship but I don't know what the outcome was.
R: My second question is will they give me a job at the end of the internship?
P: That depends on your academic record, how well you do and whether they have any vacancies!
R: OK, thanks professor for your help and advice.

习惯用语 1

① the legalities: 合法性   ③ written evidence: 书面证据
② minimum wage: 最低工资

R: 您好，我是一名大学生，想准备实习，别人说向您咨询有关学生实习的法律方面的问题是最好的。
P: 嗯，我是人民大学法律系的教授，所以知道一些情况。你想知道什么？
R: 第一个问题是实习时我有获得报酬的权利吗？
P: 劳动法上并没有详细的相关规定。学生是一个特殊的群体，他们的劳动不被视为真正的雇用。这就是说他们没有最低工资保障和保险。所以可能有的公司根本不提供报酬或仅仅提供午饭和交通费。
R: 那在我看来，实习生就是个廉价劳动力啊。他们为什么不支付工资？
P: 嗯，一些公司认为他们为学生提供了软件和硬件方面的环境，供他们实践从课本上所学到的知识，但是学生们仅仅是在使用公司的资源并不能为公司做出任何贡献。
R: 我明白学生可以从实践中获取经验，但我还是觉得他们应该得到报酬。
P: 我认为最好是在你开始工作之前确定你是否会得到报酬。那样你就可以做出决定。毕竟，你可以获得宝贵的实践经验，并且还有可能得到一份工作。
R: 要是公司一开始承诺给我实习报酬，但最终又拒绝支付，我该怎么办？

P: 除非你签了合同或者有字据，否则在法庭上可能很难证明。我知道浙江大学的一名学生最近因为公司没有支付他实习费而起诉了他所在的实习单位，但我不知道结果如何。
R: 第二个问题是，实习期结束后他们会提供我一份工作吗？
P: 这取决于你的学习成绩、实习期的表现以及他们的职位是否有空缺！
R: 好，谢谢您的帮助和建议。

Questions 1

1. Do you think interns should be paid?
2. Would you do an internship without pay?

Dialogue 2

Lucy: I've been trying to get an internship but so far I've had no luck. The problem is that I don't know anybody and who's going to accept me as an intern if they don't know me?

Mary: You could try the Student Employment Service on campus.

L: I never thought of that. Thanks. What else can I do?

M: You could try **networking**①. Start with the people around you—parents, professors, friends. I got my first part-time job—as an assistant editor, which **turned out**② to be one of my most memorable experiences—through my tutor.

L: OK, I'll give that a try. Any other suggestions?

M: Try sending your résumé to as many companies as possible.

L: I've done that but I've not had any response.

M: Perhaps there is something wrong with your résumé. You should get one of your English teachers to check it for you.

L: Yeah, that might be it. Maybe I've made some silly mistakes in my English!

M: And another thing! Once you've corrected your résumé you could take some copies with you and go and see the HR manager of some companies. Seeing them in person might help.

L: Thanks Mary. I'll go and see Nick my English teacher now. He's always so helpful.

M: Good luck!

习惯用语 2

① networking: 关系网（通过朋友、同事和熟人获得社交、事业或商业上的优势）
② turn out: 最后成为

L: 我一直在努力找实习工作但是目前还没找到。问题在于我不认识任何人，如果他们都不认识我，怎么会有人接收我实习呢？

M: 你可以去学校里的学生就业服务中心看看。

L: 你不说，我倒把这个给忘了。谢谢。我还能做些什么？

M: 你可以通过关系网。从你身边的人开始——父母、老师、朋友。我的第一份兼职工作是助理编辑，那是我最难忘的经历之一，那就是通过我的导师得到的。

L: 好，我会试试的。还有别的建议吗？

M: 尽可能多地向各家公司投递简历。

L: 我投了，但是没有任何回复。

M: 也许是你的简历有什么问题。你应该找位英语老师帮你检查一下。

L: 是，有可能。也许我犯了一些低级错误！

M: 还有一点！一旦你修改好了简历上的错误，你可以带几份复印件去见一些公司的人力资源部经理。亲自会见可能会有帮助。

L: 谢谢你，Mary。我现在就去找我的英语老师 Nick。他总是乐于助人。

M: 祝你好运！

Questions 2

1. How will you go about getting an internship?
2. Have you had your résumé proofread by an English teacher?

Dialogue 3

Tom: Hi Lucy. Congratulations on getting that internship. How's it going?

Lucy: Great Tom thanks. It was tough at first as I had to **learn the ropes**① but now it's going well.

T: So, what was difficult about it at first?

L: My first assignment was to make phone calls to potential clients.

T: That's called **cold-calling**②, isn't it?

L: That's right! Many of the people I spoke to weren't aware of the services my company was offering and because I was a novice I didn't know much either.

T: Sounds tough! So what did you do?

L: I asked my colleagues to recommend some reading material and then I spent a couple of days and nights reading them, making notes and asking lots of questions.

T: Sounds like you were back in school!

L: Yeah! But my efforts **paid off**③ because I could pass on my **new-found**④ knowledge and the result was that some clients **bought in**⑤ to our services.

T: Great! So do you think that you will work for them when you graduate?

L: It's a strong possibility. They're pleased with me and I'm happy there. As I've got **one foot in the door**⑥ I'm hoping they'll offer me a permanent job once the internship is over.

T: I'm sure they will. Anyway, good luck!

L: Thanks Tom.

习惯用语 3

① learn the ropes：摸清门路，掌握窍门
② cold-calling：冷不防打电话（无事先接触或缘由径自打电话给潜在客户推销商品）
③ pay off：成功了
④ new-found：最近，最新的
⑤ buy in：为自己买得某种身份
⑥ one foot in the door：一只脚已经在门里了（获得进入公司或行业的机会）

T：嗨，Lucy。恭喜你得到了那份实习工作。感觉怎么样？

L：很好，Tom，谢谢你。刚开始在摸索的时候很难，但是现在都进行得顺利了。

T：那开始的时候有什么困难呢？

L：我开始的工作是给所有的潜在客户打电话。

T：就是冷不防给那些潜在客户打电话，对吧？

L：对！大部分接电话的人根本不知道我们公司提供的服务，由于我是个新手，我也不太了解。

T：听起来很艰难啊！那你怎么做的呢？

L：我请我的同事推荐了一些说明材料，然后花了几天几夜时间来看，做记录，请教了好多问题。

T：听起来你好像又回到了学校！

L：是的！但是我的努力得到了回报，因为我把新的知识讲给客户听，结果有一些客户就被说动了，开始使用了我们的服务。

T：太好了！那你毕业以后会不会就留在那儿工作了呢？

L：很有可能。他们对我很满意，我在这儿也很开心。既然我已经一只脚跨进了门槛，我希望实习结束的时候公司会给我一个全职职位。

T：我相信会的。不管怎样，祝你好运！

L：谢谢 Tom！

Questions 3

1. If you come across difficulties in your internship what would you do?
2. Do you apply for internships in the hope of getting a job there or are you more interested in gathering experience?

Chapter 10　Career 事业

38　兼职工作
Part-time Jobs

Background Information

Many students have part-time jobs. Not only do they help their finances but they give them valuable work experiences too. The minimum wage for part-time jobs in Beijing is 7.9 yuan an hour. In 2005, the Education Ministry issued guidelines for part-time student work. The guidelines state that students should be paid no less than 8 yuan per hour and should work no more than eight hours per week.

A survey of about 500 students at 14 universities in Beijing by the China Foundation for Alleviating Poverty found that 80% of students from poor families who don't return home for winter vacation do part-time jobs. Around 40% of these said they had some experience of being cheated.

大部分学生都有兼职工作。兼职不仅可以挣钱而且还可以获得宝贵的工作经验。在北京兼职的最低薪水是每小时7.9元。2005年教育部为学生兼职工作下达了指导方针。方针指出，学生工资不得少于每小时8元，一周工作不得超过8小时。

中国扶贫基金会针对来自于北京14所大学的约500名学生进行的调查显示，80%贫困家庭的学生寒假都不返家而留下做兼职工作。他们当中40%的人都称曾经有过受骗的遭遇。

背景信息

Dialogue 1

Lisa: I really want to find a part-time job teaching Chinese. Have you any suggestions?

Wendy: You could try putting a poster up at Beijing Language and Culture University. There's always a lot of foreigners who want to learn Chinese there and the fact that you're an English major will be a great asset.

L: That's a good idea. Do you know what **the going rate**[①] is for an hour?

W: I believe it's 20 yuan. But why don't you have a look at some of the posters first? That way you can **size up the opposition**[②], see what makes an attractive poster and find the best sites to put up your posters.

L: You're so full of good ideas. Any more?

W: Putting posters up is a bit passive. You could try to be more proactive by producing a **flyer**[③] and handing them out to every foreigner you meet.

L: Another great idea! What next?

W: You need to find somewhere quiet for teaching. Whatever you do, don't go back to a foreigner's dorm unless they are female.

L: Why?

W: Some foreigners are more interested in romance than learning Chinese so you don't want to find yourself **in an awkward situation**[④].

L: I never thought of that. You are so sensible! I'll go to BLCU now.

W: Good luck!

习惯用语 1

① the going rate: 现行工资水平，现行的价位
② size up the opposition: 评估对手是什么情况
③ flyer: 分发的广告传单
④ in an awkward situation: 处境很尴尬

L: 我真想找一份教中文的兼职工作。你有什么建议吗？
W: 你可以试试在北京语言大学招贴海报。那儿经常有很多想学中文的外国人，你是英语专业的学生，这是最大的优势。
L: 好主意。你知道一小时通常能挣多少钱吗？
W: 我认为是20元。你可以先看看其他的招贴海报对工资的要求啊，也了解一下对手的情况，看如何做出吸引人的招贴海报，找到最好的地方贴你的海报。
L: 你的好主意真多。还有吗？
W: 光贴海报有点儿被动。你可以更主动点儿，做一些传单发给每个你遇到的外国人。
L: 又一个好主意！接下来呢？
W: 你要找个安静的地方教学。无论如何，不要去老外的宿舍，除非对方是个女生。
L: 为什么？
W: 因为一些外国人对风流韵事比对学习中文更有兴趣，你也不想让自己陷入尴尬的境地吧。
L: 我从没想过这个。你真明智！我现在要去北京语言大学。
W: 祝你好运！

Questions 1

1. Have you ever had a part-time job teaching Chinese? What did you like or not like about it?
2. How did you find your clients?

Dialogue 2

Denny: You know I've been looking for a part-time job recently.
Will: Haven't we all! How did you get on?
D: Well I saw a hotel advertisement for part-time waiters on the campus **bulletin board**①. So I applied and got the job.
W: Great! So how's it going?
D: Not at all. That's the problem!

W: Well tell me then! Don't **keep me in suspense**②!

D: I had to pay 300 yuan as a deposit for the uniform and was told to report for work in four days' time.

W: And?

D: The manager and his secretary had disappeared. And so it seems has my money!

W: No job and 300 yuan **out of pocket**③! There's a lot of rogues preying on students these days it seems.

D: I think I'm going to stick to tutoring in future. I'm less likely to be cheated that way!

W: Good idea! Why don't we post an ad for English tutors on the Internet? I'm sure we can find a job easily enough.

D: Let's **strike while the iron's hot**④ and do it now!

习惯用语 2

① bulletin board: 布告板，布告牌
② keep sb. in suspense: 让某人一直等一个答案
③ out of pocket: 付出去的钱不能收回了
④ strike while the iron's hot: 趁热打铁，现在就做某事

D: 你知道吗，我最近一直在找兼职工作。

W: 可不是嘛，大家都在找，你找得怎么样了？

D: 我看见校园布告板上有一则酒店的广告，要招聘兼职服务生。所以我应聘并得到了这份工作。

W: 太好了！那工作怎么样？

D: 一点儿也不好。这就是问题的所在！

W: 那告诉我啊！别让我着急啦！

D: 我得先交300元钱作为制服的押金，并通知我4天后去报到上班。

W: 然后呢？

D: 经理和他的秘书都消失了。因此我的钱也消失了！

W: 没有了工作，300元钱也打了水漂！现在似乎有很多骗子专骗学生的钱。

D: 我打算以后就找家教的工作了。那样我不太容易被骗！
W: 好主意！我们干嘛不在网上发布英语家教的广告呢。我相信我们可以轻松地找到兼职工作。
D: 让我们打铁趁热，现在就开始做吧！

> **Questions 2**
> 1. Have you ever been cheated like this?
> 2. What did you do?

Dialogue 3

Julia: Hi Maggie, I've just come back from my part-time job teaching English.

Maggie: What's it like?

J: Well, I tutor a nine-year-old boy and I go to his house twice a week. He's **really keen on**① learning English and his parents are very nice. What about you? How's your tutoring going?

M: At first the father **picked me up**② as it's far away but then he said he'd meet me at the gate of his compound.

J: That's bad. So what did you do?

M: I got him to pay me an extra 20 yuan for the bus fare and the travelling time.

J: That's OK then. What's the kid like?

M: It was difficult at first because he didn't like to study so we did some English games and now he's a bit more interested in English.

J: Do you want to be an English teacher when you graduate?

M: I think I'd rather work for a multi-national company. What about you?

J: I'd like to be a teacher. The pay's OK and the holidays are long!

M: That's because you're a lazy student! I think you'd soon find out that teaching involves a lot of work and responsibility!
J: Well in that case I think I'll join you in a multi-national company!

习惯用语 3

① really keen on: 非常喜爱　　② pick sb. up: 开车接某人

J: 嗨 Maggie，我刚做完教英语的兼职回来。
M: 觉得怎么样？
J: 嗯，我教一个 9 岁的小男孩，每周去他家两次。他非常喜欢学英语，他的父母也很和蔼。你呢？你的家教怎么样？
M: 因路程远，起初那家的父亲开车接我过去，但后来他就改成在他家小区门口等我了。
J: 太糟了。那你怎么做的呢？
M: 我要他为公交车费和路上浪费的时间额外付我 20 元。
J: 那还差不多。小孩怎么样？
M: 开始很困难，因为他根本不喜欢学习，所以我们就做一些英语游戏，现在他对英语有点儿兴趣了。
J: 你毕业了想做英语老师吗？
M: 我想我更喜欢去跨国公司工作。你呢？
J: 我想当老师。薪水还可以假期也长！
M: 因为你就是个懒学生！我想你很快就会发现教学工作其实很繁重而且还要承担责任。
J: 嗯，那样的话我想我也要和你一样进跨国公司工作了！

Questions 3

1. Do you like tutoring?
2. Would you like to be an English teacher when you graduate? Why? Why not?

Chapter 10 Career 事业

39 边上学边做生意
Running a Part-time Business

Background Information

Many students use their time at university to start their own business. This can range from selling dictionaries to discount cards, from sandwiches to software, from phone cards to plants, from fruit to fashionable clothes. Students are at that time of life when they are full of energy, have plenty of time and have a captive customer base.

许多大学生都利用自己的课余时间开始经商做买卖。从卖字典到打折卡，从三明治到软件，从电话卡到绿色植物，从水果到时装。大学期间正是学生们精力旺盛的时候，他们有足够的时间和忠实的客户群。

背景信息

Dialogue 1

Abbie: Hi Sally. I'm thinking of starting my own business here on campus. Any ideas?

Sally: As a student majoring in business I think that's a great idea. I think you should consider first of all doing something that you are interested in or there is a market for.

A: I can't really think of anything **off the top of my head**① now.

S: Let me tell you a true story. Two girls at Zhejiang University of Media and Communications started a "sky snack bar" in their dorm. They would supply hot instant noodles, biscuits and drinks from 8 pm until 1 am.

A: But how did they get customers?

S: They opened a QQ account and advertised on the Q-zone and this way they got instant orders from their dorm.

A: But how could they make it pay if the service was only open in their dorm?

S: Well their prices were a little higher than the supermarket but business was so good that they made a profit of 1,000 yuan in a two-month period.

A: Wow, that's impressive!

S: That's not all. They're thinking of extending their service to other dorms too.

A: They're real entrepreneurs! I'm sure that when they graduate they'll start their own full-time business!

S: That's one of the advantages of running a part-time business at college because it gives you valuable experience and **know-how**② that you can transfer to another business later.

A: I'd better **put on my thinking hat**③ and try to think of a business that I can start!

习惯用语 1

① off the top of sb.'s head: 不假思索地
② know-how: 窍门，技巧，实际知识
③ put on sb.'s thinking hat: 思考状态，专注思考

A: 嗨 Sally。我正考虑在校园里开始我的小生意呢。你有什么主意吗？
S: 对于一个商学专业的学生来说，我觉得做生意是个好主意。我认为你首先应该考虑做的是你感兴趣的，或者有市场前景的东西。
A: 我现在还真的什么都想不出来。
S: 我给你讲个真实的故事。两名浙江传媒学院的女孩在她们的宿舍经营了一个"天空快餐吧"。她们从晚8点至凌晨1点提供热的方便面、饼干和饮料。
A: 但是他们怎么招揽顾客呢？
S: 她们开了个 QQ 账户，在 Q-zone 上发布广告，她们用这种方式，很快就有顾客从她们宿舍订餐了。
A: 但是她们只在宿舍里提供服务怎么能盈利呢？
S: 嗯，她们的价格比超市贵一点，但是生意很好，她们两个月就盈利 1000 元钱。
A: 哇，相当不错！
S: 不仅如此。她们正考虑把服务扩张到其他宿舍。
A: 真是企业家啊！我相信她们毕业了将会开展全职的生意！
S: 这是大学里做兼职生意的好处，因为你可以获得有价值的经验和实际知识。以后可以将这些经验移植到其他生意上去。
A: 我好好考虑一下，想想我可以着手哪种生意！

Questions 1

1. Can you think of a part-time business that you can run?
2. What are the advantages and disadvantages?

Dialogue 2

Amanda: Hi Lily. How's your shop going?
Lily: Very well. We **made a profit**① in the first month!

A: What made you decide on a sandwich shop in the first place?

L: My boyfriend and I were sitting in a Subway shop when I suddenly thought, "Why not open my own shop since I like sandwiches so much!"

A: What were your biggest problems to begin with?

L: Rent! So expensive! I finally found a small shop about 4 square metres near several universities. You know that location, location, location are the three most important things!

A: As an advertising major you would know that! Any other problems?

L: Money! I have none and neither has my boyfriend so I had to borrow 20,000 yuan from my parents for the **start-up capital**②.

A: That was kind of them. They must really believe in you. What's the secret of your success?

L: Two things. My sandwiches are half the price of Subway's. Second, I always smile at my customers. I like to make them feel welcome.

A: How do you manage your studies and the shop?

L: My boyfriend helps out and I have some friends who work part-time for me. So my studies don't suffer too much.

A: What about the future?

L: Obviously I'd like to have a chain of shops just like Subway!

A: I'm sure you will. Good luck!

习惯用语 2

① make a profit: 获利，有利润　　② start-up capital: 启动资金

A: 嗨 Lily。你的店怎么样了？

L: 非常好。我们第一个月就盈利了！

A: 是什么让你决定开一间三明治店呢?
L: 我和男朋友当时正坐在"赛百味"快餐店里,我突然想到:"既然我这么喜欢吃三明治,为什么不自己开家店呢!"
A: 开始时最大的问题是什么?
L: 租金!太贵了!我最后找到了一个大约4平米的小店,紧挨着几所大学。你知道最重要的三个要素是:地段、地段、还是地段!
A: 你是学广告的,肯定知道这点!还有什么别的问题吗?
L: 钱!我什么钱都没有,我男朋友也是,所以我不得不跟我父母借了2万元作为启动资金。
A: 他们太好了。肯定是很信任你。那你的成功秘诀是什么呢?
L: 两个。我的三明治价格是"赛百味"的一半。第二,对顾客我总是面带微笑。我想让他们感觉到自己是受欢迎的。
A: 你怎么兼顾学习和小店的经营呢?
L: 我男朋友帮我,我有些朋友还给我做兼职。所以并不会太耽误我的学习。
A: 将来有什么打算呢?
L: 我当然想像"赛百味"一样开连锁店了!
A: 我相信你会的。祝你好运!

Questions 2

1. What are some commodities that you could provide for fellow students at a cheaper price?
2. How would you raise your start-up capital?

Dialogue 3

Wayne: Your IT company is doing very well. How did you first **get started**[①]?

Paul: Thanks. I've always been interested in electronics and since I major in Telecommunications here at BUPT I can **keep up-to-date with**[②] the latest products. My roommates noticed that I always had the latest model so they asked me to buy one for them. It just **snow-balled**③ from there.

W: Can you give me a specific example?

P: In my first year I noticed a large demand on campus for mobile phone data wires so I got in touch with an electronics corporation in Guangdong and became their agent.

W: I see. Your first customers were your roommates and then how did it spread?

P: Well, my roommates told their classmates and friends and soon I was getting so many calls that I had to rent an office and install a **land-line**④.

W: What products do you offer?

P: I'm now an agent for more than 10 companies so I can offer **a wide range of**⑤ goods and I always try to **tailor-make**⑥ a product for each customer.

W: What are the advantages for you of running an IT company?

P: Obviously I, my family and friends get electronic goods at a lower price and I can provide part-time jobs for students on campus?

W: What makes a good salesman, do you think?

P: Selling is not only a skill you can learn but it's also an attitude. An attitude where you **put yourself in other people's shoes**⑦ and see things from their perspective.

W: Great! So what product would you suggest for me!

习惯用语 3

① get start: 开始
② keep up-to-date with: 了解最新进展或消息
③ snow-ball: 滚雪球般增长
④ land-line: 固定电话
⑤ a wide range of: 各种各样的
⑥ tailor-make: 量身制作
⑦ put oneself in other people's shoes: 设身处地为别人着想，从其他人的角度看某事

W: 你的IT公司做得确实不错。你是怎么开始的呢?
P: 谢谢。我一直对电子学很感兴趣,由于我是在北京邮电大学学通信工程的,我可以一直接触最新的产品。我的室友注意到我总是有最新型的产品,所以他们叫我也给他们买。从那儿开始生意就一步步增多了。
W: 能举个具体的例子吗?
P: 第一年我注意到学校里对手机数据线的需求量很大,所以我联系了一家广东的电子公司,并成为他们的代理。
W: 我知道了。你第一批客户就是你的室友,那你是如何拓展客源的呢?
P: 嗯,我的室友告诉他们的同学和朋友,很快我就接到很多电话,我不得不租一间办公室并安装一部座机。
W: 你都卖些什么产品呢?
P: 我现在是十余家公司的代理,所以我能提供很多种类的产品,我总是努力为每个客户量身选择适合他们的产品。
W: 经营一家IT公司对你有什么好处吗?
P: 当然了,我、我的家人和朋友都可以低价买到电子产品。我也可以给学校的学生提供兼职工作。
W: 你认为怎么才能成为一名优秀的推销员?
P: 销售不仅需要那些你可以学到的技巧,还要靠态度。你要设身处地的从他们的角度考虑问题。
W: 太好了!那你给我推荐什么产品呢!

Questions 3

1. What are some products that are in big demand among students on your campus?
2. Which products would you choose and how would you start your own business?

Chapter 10　Career 事业

40　找工作
Finding a Job

Background Information

In 2006 4.13 million students graduated but there were only 1.66 million jobs available. In Beijing over 75% of university graduates prefer to stay in the city according to a recent *Capital Development Report*. It also found that 40% of graduates expect to earn 2,000 to 3,000 yuan per month. A survey in early 2007 by academics from Peking, Tsinghua and China Political Science and Law universities found that 85% of job-hunters believed that there is discrimination in employment and that 58% think the problem is severe. Most discrimination involves appearance, lack of height, state of health, marital status, permanent residency and gender. Most graduates have to submit 42 résumés on average to get a job according to a 2007 Beijing Academy of Social Sciences report.

2006年，413万学生毕业，但社会仅仅可以提供166万个工作职位。根据最新一期的《首都发展报告》显示，在北京，75%以上的大学毕业生更愿意留京发展，且40%以上毕业生期望月薪在2000—3000元。2007年初，由北京大学、清华大学、中国政法大学联合进行的一项调查发现，85%求职者认为就业存在歧视，58%的人认为歧视问题十分严重。歧视主要体现在外貌、身高、健康状况、婚姻情况、户口和性别方面。根据2007年北京社会科学研究院的报告，大部分毕业生获得一份工作平均需要投递42份简历。

背景信息

Dialogue 1

Jessica: Hi Amy, how's the job-hunting going?

Amy: It's really tough going. Most jobs require you to have experience which I don't have. It's a real **catch-22 situation**①. I need experience to get a job but without a job I can't get experience!

J: Well, you've still got several months to go before you graduate so don't give up yet!

A: I won't but I'm also considering whether to stay on and **do a master's**②.

J: But there's no guarantee that with a master's you'll get a job.

A: I know, but I'm hoping the job market will have improved by then.

J: Personally, I think it's better to get a job now because work experience is so vital. Just think, in 3 years time you could have a good job with a big salary or a master's with no job. It's a **no-brainer**③!

A: Maybe you're right. I'd better re-double my job-hunting efforts.

J: Why don't we practice some job interviews? I could be the interviewer.

A: Great idea! We need to work out some questions together so that I can prepare some answers.

J: Let's go for a coffee and think of some.

A: Yeah, let's go.

习惯用语 1

① catch-22 situation: 令人左右为难的规定（或情况）
② do a master's: 读研究生，攻读硕士学位
③ no-brainer: 不需要用智力或思考

J: 嗨 Amy，工作找得怎么样了？
A: 真的太困难了。大部分职位都要求你有工作经验，但是我没有。真是令人左右为难。我需要有工作经验才能找到工作，但是没有工作我就没法有工作经验！
J: 嗯，离毕业还有几个月的时间呢，所以不要放弃！
A: 我不会放弃但是我也在考虑是继续找工作还是读研究生。
J: 但是硕士毕业也不能保证你能找到工作啊。
A: 我知道，但是我希望那时候就业情况能有所改善。
J: 我个人认为现在就工作比较好，因为工作经验是至关重要的。想一想3年后，你是想有一份挣很多钱的好工作，还是想光有硕士学位而没有工作，这还用考虑吗？
A: 可能你是对的。我最好加倍努力找工作了。
J: 我们为什么不实践一些工作面试？我可以当面试官。
A: 好主意！我们要一起设计一些问题以便我准备答案。
J: 我们去喝点儿咖啡好好考虑一下。
A: 嗯，走吧。

Questions 1

1. Are you finding it difficult to get a job?
2. What are the advantages and disadvantages of post-graduate studies?
3. Do you think that practicing interviews is a good idea?

Dialogue 2

Jessica: Well, Amy any luck?
Amy: I've had several interviews but nothing so far.
J: How did they go?
A: One interviewer said they were only employing males so that was a waste of time!
J: It's terrible that there's so much **sexual discrimination**[①] these days! After all we're equal now. Didn't Chairman Mao say we **hold up half the sky**[②]!

A: I know but try telling some employers that! They think that girls will leave when they get married or move to another city with their boyfriend.
J: That's so old-fashioned!
A: And another kept making **sexual innuendo's**③ so I wouldn't work there at any price!
J: Some employers only want to hire pretty girls for obvious reasons!
A: Sometimes I'm glad that I'm not pretty! That way companies have to judge me on my ability and not looks!
J: You'll find something soon. Keep looking!

习惯用语 2

① sexual discrimination: 性别歧视
② hole up half the sky: 平等，能顶半边天
③ sexual innuendo's: 通过旁敲侧击的方式谈论有关性的问题

J: Amy，有什么收获吗？
A: 我已经面试了好几次了，但是目前还没结果。
J: 都是怎么回事？
A: 一位面试官说他们只想招聘男生，所以那只是浪费时间！
J: 真糟糕，现在性别歧视竟然如此泛滥！毕竟我们现在都是男女平等啊。毛主席不是说过我们能顶半边天嘛！
A: 我知道，可那些老板谁听这个啊。他们认为女孩一旦结婚就会离职或者跟男朋友去别的城市。
J: 思想太过时了！
A: 还有一个公司，在面试时，一直暗示关于性的问题，所以给我多少钱我也不会在那儿工作！
J: 有些老板只想雇漂亮的女孩，原因很明显！
A: 有时候我很庆幸自己不漂亮！这样公司就会根据我的能力而不是外貌来做出判断。
J: 你很快就会找到工作的。继续找！

> **Questions 2**
> 1. Have you faced any sex discrimination in applying for jobs?
> 2. What did you do?

Dialogue 3

Amy: I'm so desperate for a job that I tried an agency the other day.

Jessica: You want to be careful! I've heard some horror stories about agencies.

A: You don't have to tell me! This agency wanted 6,000 yuan as a **down payment**① and another 6,000 if I got a job.

J: Wow, that's a lot of money! What do they offer for that?

A: They said they would give me four months of training. There's about 30 students in the class and we get to train with different companies.

J: It's still a lot of money to **shell out**② and there's no guarantee of a job at the end of it.

A: I think so too so I'm going to try some more agencies today.

J: What about going West?

A: You mean America?

J: No. I mean West China. The government is encouraging students to apply for junior village official positions.

A: I thought about that but I heard that 30,000 applied for just 3,000 jobs!

J: But it's worth it because they guarantee a salary of 2,000 yuan for the first year. And students who complete three years are given priority for local government jobs.

A: I've thought about that but maybe the living conditions are not so good. And the night life will be non-existent!

J: You're too used to Beijing, that's your problem!

习惯用语 3

① down payment: 首付　　　② shell out: 支付

A: 我急着要找工作，所以那天去了一家中介。
J: 你一定要小心！关于中介我听说过一些很恐怖的故事。
A: 你不用说了！这个中介要我首付 6000 元钱，如果找到工作要再付 6000 元。
J: 哇，要这么多钱！他们凭什么要这么多？
A: 他们说他们会安排我参加四个月的培训。一个班大约 30 个人，我们在不同的公司培训。
J: 还要交一大笔钱，而且最后还不保证一定有工作。
A: 我也这么想，所以我打算今天去更多的中介试试。
J: 去西部怎么样？
A: 你是说美国？
J: 不是，我是说中国西部。政府鼓励学生申请乡村基层的职位。
A: 我考虑过，但是我听说三万人竞争三千个职位！
J: 但还是值得一试，因为政府保证第一年有 2000 元的工资。工作三年后优先选择当地政府的职位。
A: 我考虑了这个，但是生活条件可能不是很好。而且夜生活就根本不存在了！
J: 你在北京待习惯了，这才是你的问题！

Questions 3

1. Have you ever tried a job agency?
2. Would you consider working in the countryside for three years?

Career 事业

图书在版编目（CIP）数据

嘻哈口语大话校园／（英）斯特克（Stirk, N.）著；
张满胜译．——北京：外文出版社，2007
（英语国际人）
ISBN 978-7-119-04871-0

Ⅰ．嘻… Ⅱ．① 斯… ② 张… Ⅲ．英语-口语 Ⅳ. H319.9

中国版本图书馆 CIP 数据核字（2007）第 115580 号

英语国际人
嘻哈口语大话校园

作　　者	Nick Stirk（英）
策　　划	蔡　箐
责任编辑	李春英
封面设计	红十月设计室
印刷监制	冯　浩

ⓒ外文出版社
出版发行　外文出版社
地　　址　中国北京西城区百万庄大街24号　　邮政编码　100037
网　　址　http://www.flp.com.cn
电　　话　（010）68995964/68995883（编辑部）
　　　　　（010）68320579/68996067（总编室）
　　　　　（010）68995844/68995852（发行部/门市邮购）
　　　　　（010）68327750/68996164（版权部）
电子信箱　info@flp.com.cn/sales@flp.com.cn
印　　制　北京飞达印刷有限责任公司
经　　销　新华书店/外文书店
开　　本　大 32 开　　　　　　　　　印　张　8.625
印　　数　00001-10000 册　　　　　字　数　180 千字
装　　别　平
版　　次　2007 年第 1 版第 1 次印刷
书　　号　ISBN 978-7-119-04871-0
定　　价　16.00 元

外文社图书　版权所有　侵权必究
外文社图书　有印装错误可随时退换